COLLATERAL DAMAGE

The unintended victims of crime

COLLATERAL DAMAGE

ROBIN BOWLES

 LAKE PRESS

 **LAKE PRESS**

Lake Press Pty Ltd
5 Burwood Road
Hawthorn VIC 3122 Australia
www.lakepress.com.au

Printed in Australia by
McPhersons Printing Group 5 4 3 2 1
LP21 246

 A catalogue record for this
book is available from the
National Library of Australia

DEDICATION

To my patient and conscientious editor, Jenny Lee, who has travelled many millions of words, debated accuracies and legalese and sometimes held tense discussions with me over inclusions and exclusions over the past twenty-four years. (She always wins!) She spends many hours turning my scribbles into the books you hold. A good editor is a writer's best friend and Jenny is the best. Thank you, Jenny, for being with me all the way.

ACKNOWLEDGEMENTS

Books about real people always involve the support and trust of many protagonists. First, thanks to the people whose stories appear in this book. To have their trust that I will be able to tell their stories and share the pain of baring very intimate feelings and sometimes secrets gives me a great sense of humility. Thank you to all who have felt brave enough to put their stories in my care.

A big thanks also to the many members of the professions encircling the wide world of true crime – pathologists, forensic scientists, police, legal advisers and others – who have agreed to discuss their involvement with me and been open about their roles in dealing with the crimes discussed here. It is not only the living victims who become collateral damage in these crimes; the burden of investigating some cases has ongoing effects on the investigators as well.

To my editor Jenny Lee and all at Lake Press who had faith in the need for a book of this nature to be published, thank you.

And last but not least, big thanks to my husband Clive, who knows the drill by now and doesn't expect dinner on time while I'm writing, and also to Chewie, my little dog, who lies in her bed at my feet, waiting ... waiting. Will the *next* time I stand up mean a walk?

And to you, dear readers, another one for your bookshelves – collect the whole set and let me know what you think!

Robin Bowles
Melbourne
robinbowles@bigpond.com

CONTENTS

INTRODUCTION

Over almost a quarter of a century, many people have shared stories with me about the most traumatic event in their lives. Deaths of loved ones in horrific circumstances, unjust prison sentences, kidnappings, murders, untrue allegations ruining lives and more of the horrors some unfortunate people get thrown at them.

This collection of stories has grown over the past few years from my many encounters with people in the depths of despair, sometimes without any outlet except being able to talk to someone like me. They are important stories and should be told.

I've assembled a collection here that reflects the many terrible things that can happen to ordinary people. Most of the individuals here aren't gangsters or murderers, but ordinary people who were living ordinary lives when something extraordinary happened to them and they lost control of their destinies.

'Police Line – Do Not Cross' is the story of Joe D'Alo, a young, career-minded cop, showing how the trajectory of our lives can suddenly shift from success to the depths of disgrace. Joe fell from grace because he took pride in his job; he wrote a book describing how the murders of two of his colleagues, Gary Silk and Rod Miller, had been patiently investigated with great dedication and skill over more than four years. His reward was to be silenced and sidelined by the police machine. The Silk–Miller murders affected hundreds of people, and Joe D'Alo was one of them.

'Kissing Toads' is a collection of vignettes based on stories I've been told by women who have become involved in the criminal world, sometimes breaking the law themselves but more often falling for men who have. Love causes people to act strangely at times, as these women's stories show. Some women have gone to extraordinary lengths in order to hang on to their men.

Others unwittingly walk into relationships with men who are leading dual lives. Respectable and caring on the surface, in secret they're committing terrible crimes. One woman in this situation is Josie, whose story is told in 'He Was So Beautiful'. She was, in her own words, 'just a simple Italian girl' who met a stranger on a dating service. She thought she would help him kick his cannabis habit, but she later discovered his habits were much worse than that.

Many Tasmanians know the name of Karen Keefe, but she is less well known on the mainland. Karen was a minor but important player in the drama of Sue Neill-Fraser, who was convicted of murdering her partner Bob Chappell. Sue has been incarcerated since August 2009 and remains in jail despite the fact that, in 2017, a witness named Meaghan Vass came forward to say that she and two men were on the boat that night, and Sue Neill-Fraser was not. Meaghan's evidence was broadcast on *60 Minutes* everywhere except Tasmania. The reason she broke her silence after all those years was that she was persuaded to do so by her friend Karen Keefe, who had befriended Sue Neill-Fraser in jail. In Karen's words, 'Sue was the only innocent girl in there', and Karen wanted to help her. But the Meaghan Vass account didn't suit the police story, so police set out to discredit both Meaghan and Karen. Police have spent years harassing Karen, trying to discredit her. Tasmania still shows unpleasant signs of its heritage as a penal colony!

'The Vanishing Evidence' is Noel Han's story. Noel is a slightly built Australian man of Chinese descent who was convicted of viciously murdering a friend and workmate, who was found moribund in his own apartment. The only forensics that could have cleared Noel or linked him to the crime were some hairs that were found in the apartment and later lost by the prosecution. Noel had visited his friend there on numerous occasions. If the hairs were his, they did put him in the apartment, but not necessarily on the day of the murder. If they belonged to someone else, the police had an alternative suspect. Noel was convinced the hairs definitely weren't his, and he repeatedly proclaimed his innocence. He served his full sentence because he refused to meet with the parole board, which would have required him to admit to the murder and show remorse if he wished to get out of jail.

His time on the outside after his release was nearly as bad as imprisonment. He even contemplated committing a crime so he could obtain accommodation and food, both of which were almost impossible for him to secure on the outside.

And last but not least is 'In Fear of his Life', the story of the Alva Beach killings in far north Queensland. This is a story in which nobody wins and some still have no answers. It involves a midnight home invasion, a lethal struggle, two deaths and a set of grieving relatives seeking answers. One minute, young Dean Webber was sound asleep in his family shack at beautiful Alva Beach, bordered by a pristine coastline seventeen kilometres from Ayr. Then his life collided with three others, and the results were fatal. Police are convinced Dean's version of events is truthful, but the grieving families think otherwise. Lives are blighted forever.

Whenever a serious crime is committed, law enforcers focus on the immediate victim and the culprit. If police know who the victim is, the information is commonly used to identify a potential killer. At first, police swarm around, asking searching questions, poking and prying, imposing themselves on the grief of the living victims. Then they are gone. The blue lights disappear, as does the blue-and-white ribbon. The stream of uniforms and suits moves on to the next drama.

But there are many more victims of every crime. These are the living victims. Usually, their stories disappear from the TV news; they're no longer seen on the front pages of the printed papers or on the news websites. They are mostly forgotten.

Organisations have been established around Australia to assist victims of crime, but they usually focus on people who were attacked, injured or damaged in some way. The living victims are rarely considered important enough to receive financial compensation for what they have endured, although some have spent thousands of dollars on legal or medical fees, or on counselling and psychological assistance. In Victoria, a study has been set up to investigate this anomaly and perhaps widen the catchment area for assistance to those who have been devastated by a sudden, unexpected incident that changed their lives forever.

Where transcripts or statements are used in this book, they may be edited for clarity and brevity but remain true to the words spoken. An asterisk beside a name the first time it is used means the person's name has been changed for privacy, but their story has not.

Finally, thank you to those who have shared their stories and to all my readers, who make the difficult task of listening to such sorrowful stories and the sometimes sad work of writing them worthwhile.

Robin Bowles
Melbourne
robinbowles@bigpond.com

For more reading:
http://www.nswbar.asn.au/docs/resources/submissions/innocence.pdf

For more stories on injustice, see my previously published books:
Rough Justice
Death on the Derwent
Also visit Dr Bob Moles's website, *Networked Knowledge* at
http://netk.net.au/

Chapter One

POLICE LINE – DO NOT CROSS

16 August 1998, 12.35 am

Blue lights swung in rhythmic circles, illuminating irregular factory rooftops and darkened advertising signs beside a weirdly empty four-lane road, where six police cars and several unmarked vehicles were skewed at odd angles along the kerb. Each blue rotation passed languidly over an inert body, jack-knifed into a V-shape on the road. The body was cordoned off by a flapping blue-and-white ribbon, with blue letters reading 'DO NOT CROSS'.

A dozen or more scruffily dressed men were moving around randomly, looking for anything, using torches to illuminate dark spaces. These unkempt individuals were plainclothes police, who had broken cover at the news that two undercover members had been attacked in the Melbourne suburb of Moorabbin. Some stood in small clumps, shaking their heads, talking quietly or swearing at the situation and the murdering bastards who had killed their mate. Although they all felt the urge to support their fallen brother, perhaps put something under his head, cover him for decency and protect him from the chill of the night, he lay alone, a crime scene awaiting investigation.

The air crackled with radio static. Sitreps (situation reports) were relayed to Intergraph, the police incident management and dispatch system; calls were put out for an ambulance and for the K9 Squad, as police called the dog squad; there were queries about the Air Wing and a request for a chopper to light the scene. Dismayed cries for help and support were disguised as impassive reports and directions. Roadblocks were initiated, and the Intergraph operator reported with ill-concealed urgency that a sergeant was on his way to help coordinate the deployment of resources.

A man from another approaching unit called out for directions because he didn't have his Melways street directory.

The man at the scene told him, 'We're in Warrigal and Cochranes with a member down, shot to the head … and we're missing another member. We're trying to find out what's going on.'

◆ ◆ ◆

Detective Sergeant Gary Silk was the dead cop on the road. His partner, Detective Senior Constable Rodney Miller, was found mortally wounded soon afterwards and was loaded into an ambulance at 12.42 am. Despite frantic efforts to save him, he died in hospital at 4.39 am on Sunday 17 August. It was later alleged that before he died he gasped out as much as he knew: 'Two. One on foot. Dark Hyundai. Get them. I'm fucked. Get them.'

The news of Miller's death, relayed on Intergraph, cemented the resolve of every member of Victoria Police to find the killers. But none of those listening that night could possibly have known the impact the murders of their fellow members would have on them. It would be four long years before the murderers were convicted, and even longer for some of the police involved, whose lives would never be the same.

◆ ◆ ◆

November 2003

'You're never really prepared for it,' said the trim, dark-haired young man who sat opposite me in a St Kilda Road cafe. 'You train for it, do the drills, learn the skills, but when it actually confronts you, you're gutted.'

Joe D'Alo remembered, 'That night when I got to the scene, I felt overwhelmed with shock and grief. I just fixated on the body lying there. I knew Silky was dead, but it seemed so callous, just leaving him on the road, lying in his own blood like that.' Five years on, his dark brown eyes glistened.

We had arranged to meet because I wanted a copy of Joe's newly published book, *One Down, One Missing*. I'd seen a TV interview with the young Italian-born cop, smart in a dark suit and snappy tie, telling viewers that he'd written a book with journalist David Astle about his involvement in the hunt for the alleged killers, Bandali Debs and Jason Roberts, who had since been convicted and put away for a very long time.

His book intrigued me. If it was indeed a true record of the investigation, I thought he was either brave or foolhardy to spill his guts about the inside workings of Victoria Police. I was keen to read it, because the way the cops go about things is always of interest to me. I'd been frustrated in my efforts to find it; every bookshop told me it was on order, but none of them actually had copies. I thought it must have sold very well. Most writers have a few spare copies of their books, so, being impatient to read it, I rang Acting Sergeant Joe D'Alo at his Fraud Squad office in St Kilda Road.

I told him of my quest and asked if I could buy a book from him, but he seemed hesitant.

'I've only got one copy at home, because it's actually been recalled,' he said softly. 'There's a bit of rewriting that had to be done.'

'Oh, damn! I don't want to read a sanitised version,' I told him. 'Could I borrow your copy?' After a bit of persuasion, during which I said I'd lend him a copy of one of my books in return, we agreed to meet in a cafe a little way from his office.

'Not right outside,' I suggested. 'And I'll bring my book in a plain brown wrapper. I wouldn't want you to be in trouble for fraternising with me, because I'm a bit *persona non grata* in some areas of your building.'

'So am I,' he said.

So here we were, swapping brown paper bags and chatting. He seemed like a nice young man. Rather like a youthful Tom Hanks. Very direct gaze, very earnest, a bit bewildered by the flurry generated by his book.

'Why did you write it?' I asked.

'We had no time for grief counselling or dealing with what civilians call post-traumatic shock.' He'd been assigned to the Lorimer Taskforce, the police name for the Silk–Miller investigation team. He said, 'Once we became part of Lorimer, we were full-on from the very next day, twelve- to sixteen-hour days, day after day, no weekends, little leave at all for nearly four years, totally immersed in catching the killers. It was like a mission. No let-up, no quarter given or asked.

'A few months after I'd been moved to the Lorimer Taskforce, my wife of sixteen years and I separated, leaving me with a five-year-old and a seven-year-old. I was torn between my kids and the job. But every time I even contemplated leaving, I remembered Gary Silk's brother Ian saying at the funeral, "I want to make a plea to the members of the police force. Please pursue this matter with dedication, thoroughness and professionalism, so that these criminals – these *bastards* – are detected, convicted and imprisoned." If it hadn't been for my parents, I would have had to pull out. But by then, I had so much knowledge about the investigation, it would have left a big hole in the team, so I moved in with Mum and Dad and they looked after the kids while I was at work.'

Which sounded like it was most of the time.

'I was finding the stress of the events and the memories of that night overwhelming at times,' he confided. 'So I saw a doctor and he advised me to write it all down. To help in coping. Just pour it out on paper. So, at every spare opportunity, I did. This became a way to deal with the difficult and frustrating phases of the inquiry. After it was all over, the passion to write this book grew to be the strongest thing I've ever felt in my life.' It was probably the most foolhardy too, I thought. He may have meant well, but we all know where that road paved with good intentions ends up.

We both walked away with our plain brown parcels. His book was one of the best true stories I've ever read and a fantastic PR instrument for Victoria Police. It described the Lorimer Taskforce's unswerving dedication, their endless frustrations and the great personal sacrifices they made in the pursuit of justice for Silk and Miller. It also provided a detailed insider's perspective on a highly sensitive operation.

Boy, I thought, is he going to cop it for being so honest!

◆ ◆ ◆

This is the story of what happened to Acting Sergeant Giuseppe (Joe) D'Alo, the pride and joy of his working-class Italian parents. He was a devoted father and a rising police officer who in thirteen years had only taken a handful of days off sick. He had a shining pride in his job and was doing his absolute best when the system turned against him because he'd dared to write a book about the great job Victoria Police had done in investigating the Silk–Miller murders.

When I think of the vast resources spent investigating Joe's case, I can't help wondering if the outcome justified the commitment of public money, the use of allegedly scarce police time, and the sacrifice of a valuable, dedicated officer.

◆ ◆ ◆

In January 2003, as a result of the Lorimer investigation, Bandali Debs (49) and Jason Roberts (22) were convicted of the Silk–Miller murders. Debs received a life sentence and Roberts was sentenced to thirty-five years. Serious charges for other crimes were still pending against Debs, but sentencing for these convictions would be fairly academic, as he was already going to die in prison.

Jason Roberts, however, was a different matter. Despite what the police and the jury considered overwhelming evidence against him, Roberts continued to protest his innocence.

By this time, Joe had assembled a comprehensive dossier on the Lorimer investigation. To assess interest in his outpourings, he approached Hardie Grant Publishing. They were very interested in what they described as a 'rare chance to enter into this dramatic chapter in … police history' and engaged journalist David Astle to transform Joe's notes into a publishable manuscript. Astle was paid the entire advance ($16,000) and Joe was to receive royalties at three per cent. If the book sold 10,000 copies (which would make it a bestseller in Australia) he stood to earn about $9000 for two years' work.

During Joe's meetings with the publisher, there was some discussion about how wise it was to write such a book while still in the job, and it was suggested that he should resign before the book was released. But Joe loved his job and decided to stay, so he set out to obtain his superiors' approval to have the book published. Police regulations weren't a major consideration. Now, this is probably a good time to mention Section 127A of the Police Regulations Act. At the time, the section read:

> *Any member of the police force who publishes or communicates, except to some person to whom he is authorised to publish or communicate it, any fact or document which comes to his knowledge or into his possession by virtue of his office and which it is his duty not to disclose shall be guilty of an offence against this Act and liable to a fine of not more than 20 penalty units.*

Like most police, Joe had only a hazy knowledge of the regulations, which weren't even studied at the police academy. (In fact, when I later approached the Ethical Standards Department (ESD) to obtain information on Section 127A, which by then had become crucial to Joe's case, the Victorian sergeant who dealt with my enquiry had to go away to look up the wording and ring me back.)

Joe believed the extensive evidence presented at the trials of Debs and Roberts had already put the story in the public arena, but he felt his book would provide a new perspective on the investigation. There were police regulations about undertaking a second job, but he didn't think they applied in this case, as the amount of money he stood to make was so small that it could hardly be considered income. (Most Australian writers don't make tea money.) While Joe was debating his future, the serious writing began.

When I later phoned Sandy Grant, MD of Hardie Grant Publishing, he told me that Joe was very keen to get the book out there, despite the possible risk to himself. Joe told Sandy that he'd read books and media articles about investigations he'd been personally involved in, and they were invariably sanitised. He knew that even senior police journalists were spoon fed by police, only publishing what the police allowed them to say. Even 'inside' stories were based on judicious leaks. Sandy remembered Joe saying, 'Journos never cross the line, because they know they'll be blackballed and lose their insider status.' I knew that was true.

In April 2003, about six weeks before the planned publication, Joe arranged to see the recently appointed Assistant Commissioner (Crime), Simon Overland, who had an honours degree in law, and made a separate appointment with his former boss, Inspector Paul Sheridan, who was now at Forensics. He told both men about the impending publication and explained to them that he'd taken steps to ensure that the book couldn't be used to compromise the killers' conviction, which was of paramount importance to him.

At Joe's urging, Hardie Grant had engaged criminal and defamation lawyer Geoffrey Gibson of Blake Dawson Waldron to review the manuscript, and Gibson had said that the book wouldn't raise any *sub judice* issues in the event of an appeal by Debs or Roberts. (Appeals are heard by judges, who are regarded as being above the influence of scribblings by us mere mortals, even though juries might be swayed.) Joe later handed Overland a letter from Gibson to this effect.

In return, Joe received several emails from Overland, none of which vetoed the project. Looking back at those emails now, it seems apparent that Overland himself, having begun his career in the Australian Federal Police, was unaware of Section 127A at the time. But the problems with that section became obvious once the manuscript was read by long-standing members of Victoria Police command.

Joe had another meeting with Paul Sheridan, after which he sent the manuscript to Crown prosecutor Jeremy Rapke QC, then Victoria's Director of Public Prosecutions, who had successfully prosecuted Debs and Roberts. On 4 April 2003, Mr Rapke told Joe that the manuscript wouldn't influence any subsequent appeal or retrial. Overland received Rapke's advice in writing the same day.

Rapke later told me he'd reviewed the MS, but his brief had been quite specific. 'I was looking especially for anything that might interfere with the forthcoming appeals of Debs and Roberts, favourably or adversely. I was not asked to endorse the book, just to check its *sub judice* issues.'

Once Joe was satisfied the Lorimer outcome would not be in jeopardy and Hardie Grant was reassured about the ramifications, the publishers made arrangements for the book's release.

An important point to note here is that once a manuscript is given to a publisher, the publishing company has a financial and proprietary interest in the document. The publisher is the licensed holder of the work, which means, in a nutshell, that they own a big slice of it. The publishers suggested to Simon Overland that he come to Hardie Grant, sign a confidentiality agreement and read the book in house, but he declined the offer.

By this time, Joe was beginning to realise that, with all these big guns having their fingers in the pie, he might be in trouble, so he asked the Police Association whether he'd contravened any police regulations. Meanwhile, Hardie Grant was still negotiating with Overland. The publishers were reluctant to allow a copy of the book to leave their premises before publication for fear that the book's contents would be exposed prematurely, but Overland eventually signed a confidentiality agreement and, on 13 May 2003, Hardie Grant agreed to send him a copy of the book.

Overland read the book promptly and immediately held 'a number of high-level discussions'. Among other things, he canvassed the possibility of taking out an injunction to prevent publication, but he rejected the idea. He considered his chances of obtaining an injunction were poor, and he was concerned that taking out an injunction would 'provide D'Alo publicity for his book'.

This seems like an odd decision, particularly from someone with qualifications in law. If an injunction was obtained, the book might get all the publicity in the world but it wouldn't be available. On the other hand, if a magistrate thought the book contained nothing worthy of an injunction, the application wouldn't succeed. Surely if police command were so concerned, they could have made a good case for an injunction?

But instead of going through the courts, police command communicated directly with Joe. On 16 May, three days before publication, Overland expressed his concern to Joe in an email which listed four areas of concern:

- Possible *sub judice* implications
- Disclosure of police methodology
- Privacy for other members identified in the manuscript, and
- Intellectual property ownership.

The memo concluded that further time was required to assess and consider the contents of the book. Accordingly, Joe's permission to publish was refused and he was warned that if he 'should proceed to publish the material, it would be without the permission of Victoria Police and that consequences were likely to apply'. There was still no specific mention of the likelihood of breaching any section of the Police Regulations Act.

Joe says he was now more confused than ever, because the previous day the Police Association lawyer, Robert O'Neill, had told him that his contract with Hardie Grant did not place him in contravention of Section 69 (failure to obey a direct command). Regardless, Joe knew he had Buckley's and no chance of stopping the release, and on 19

May 2003 *One Down, One Missing* made its first public appearance. Many of Joe's police colleagues attended the launch party, only to be reprimanded afterwards. The book sold its socks off, selling 11,500 copies in three months.

To say the shit hit the fan would be an underuse of the cliché. The media loved the story about the 'cop crossing the line' and the public loved the book. Vicpol, on the other hand, was more than cranky.

The *grands fromages* lost no time in rallying the troops against this insider, who was now very much on the outer. Acting on a formal complaint lodged by Ron Iddles, one of Homicide's most-respected senior sergeants, who was formalising complaints made to him by members of his crew, Acting Commander Steve Fontana lodged a complaint about Joe to the ESD. D'Alo did not get a copy. A complaint to ESD, especially from an acting commander, is a very serious event in the life of a serving police officer. Until it is resolved, it hangs over the member's head like a black cloud, clearly visible for miles. It made Joe feel like an untouchable.

The high-level campaign against D'Alo was gaining force. On 3 June 2003, Paul Sheridan, the former Lorimer commander, sent an email addressed to Lorimer Taskforce members and other police witnesses indicating that Joe's book was a personal account and was in no way endorsed by Victoria Police. Sheridan had always been supportive of D'Alo the man and D'Alo the cop, but he did have reservations about D'Alo the writer.

Others, however, didn't share his view. Joe received emails from many of his colleagues in the Lorimer Taskforce and elsewhere, ranging from superintendent to constable in rank, inside and outside Homicide, effusively praising his work. One wrote, 'I have no concerns and knew someone would do it, so why not you?' Another said, 'I came to the conclusion that a book was inevitable, probably from [journalists] that wouldn't tell the full tale.' Others said, 'Well done, mate. I'm proud of you, buddy' and described the book as 'A tribute to Gary and Rod … who made the ultimate sacrifice' and 'A real inspiration to young members'. But there were warning words: 'Be prepared though, as the grumblings have started' and, presciently, 'Watch your back.'

It seemed that a vocal minority had gained the ear of force command through their complaint to ESD. This group's reactions ranged from disbelief to fury, belligerence, a sense of betrayal and threats of litigation. Sheridan's phone rang so often he probably considered taking it off the hook permanently. He sought to dampen some of the emotions and channel the personal complaints he'd received by writing in his email, 'If any member wishes to provide information to ESD they should pursue the usual channels of communication'.

And some did. Those too angry to formalise complaints tried to organise protest meetings or sent poisonous emails saying things like, 'I will do everything in my power to ensure that your career has months left in it rather than years.'

One member mentioned briefly in the book, David 'Docket' Waters, formalised his hurt feelings by lodging a defamation writ against Joe D'Alo, David Astle and Hardie Grant. The defamation action achieved the result that had eluded Vicpol, and Hardie Grant withdrew the book from sale in August 2003. The action was later settled. This defamation payout alone ensured that neither D'Alo nor Astle will ever receive any royalties from the book.

Joe was shocked and hurt by the reaction from a core group of his colleagues and dispirited by the intimidation, humiliation and discrimination. With hindsight you could argue that, as an experienced copper, he should have been more aware of police regulations.

During my enquiries, a senior Lorimer member explained that one reason for his anger was that the possibility of a book had already been canvassed and rejected. He had a clear recollection of a lengthy discussion at one of the 'cabinet-style' meetings regularly presided over by Paul Sheridan. Someone said there had to be a book in this investigation, but the responses were mixed. Some were keen, but most were not. Someone mentioned they'd probably need help, most likely from a journalist. The overwhelming sentiment was that they weren't interested in lowering themselves to hobnob with a journalist to tell their story and they'd rather keep their secrets in house. The Lorimer member said that all decisions by this 'cabinet' group during the investigation (including whether a Lorimer tie should be designed and who would be eligible to wear it) were made by consensus 'in the democratic process' and were considered binding on all.

Joe disagrees. He says he has no recollection of the book discussion and it was extremely rare that all Lorimer members attended these meetings. The job went on and officers had to be somewhere else. To illustrate this, he says he was at the first discussion about the Lorimer tie, which vetoed the tie being given to 'the brass' (assistant and chief commissioners), but this decision was reversed at a later meeting, when several members were not there. Sheridan indicated that 'the brass' were disappointed by the previous decision and to ease pressure on him, the members voted to give them a tie. 'Not all decisions were made democratically,' Joe says in an ironic tone.

Another issue for the disgruntled Lorimer members was that they objected to the exposure of their personal frailties and information about their private lives. They also took exception to the way information about the victims and their families had been revealed (and so, apparently did the dead men's families).

During my readings of the book, I'd felt its real guts lay in the professionalism displayed by the investigators, the thrill and the tedium of the chase, culminating in the catching of a vicious killer who had been posing for years as an innocuous suburban tiler. And the termination of the career of his alleged young disciple. Both taken off the streets before they could kill or rob again and destroy more people's lives.

The occasional revelation about the strains felt by the individual investigators was one of the strengths of the book, like the glue holding the front story together. One for all, all for one. Joe had portrayed the tough members of the 'Hommies' as human and vulnerable; he'd explained how they'd followed thousands of hot leads that fizzled out, making dozens of unsavoury contacts to no avail. He'd vividly described the frustrations and fallout from the daily and nightly grind, which led more often than not to bitter disappointment, at which point they had to start all over again. His book gave me new insight into the work of the police and a renewed respect for its members.

But the agitators and increasingly 'the brass' saw it differently. Although Joe had laid his own private life and feelings equally bare in his book, his critics saw him as one of their own who'd betrayed them. To them, he'd breached confidences and deliberately flouted written and unwritten rules in police culture that said you should *not* write a book.

One Down, One Missing was released only a few months after Debs and Roberts were convicted. This was a sound commercial publishing decision by Hardie Grant, but many police saw the proximity of the book's release to the wrap-up of the case as too confronting. As one senior officer told me, 'These were not boys, they were men – hard, tough, handpicked men. They were furious, and we were concerned about how they may physically behave towards D'Alo on more than one occasion. It might have been better if he'd waited a while. They were all still so connected, so raw ...'

It also became apparent that the privacy of Vicpol individuals was not the only concern. The book had bluntly revealed the names of police informers, mentioned in the context of their relationships to the Lorimer investigation. Irate calls from contacts who had previously been nurtured and protected by Vicpol were more than embarrassing. In fact, the exposure was seen as downright dangerous to those who'd been identified and not inconsequential to those who'd used the information. I wasn't privy to the immediate reaction, but I'm willing to bet that cries of 'How the fuck did this happen?' resounded along the corridors of power.

Like most emotional reactions, the response of the members became disproportionate to the offence, from the bottom to the top. For example, on 2 June 2003, only three weeks after the book's release, an official Vicpol email was sent to everyone involved in Lorimer – everyone but Joe D'Alo, who heard about it on the grapevine. The email notified them that they were eligible for the Chief Commissioner's Commendation Award, which is rarely given and highly prized. The awards would be presented by the governor on 13 August (almost the fifth anniversary of the murders) in the presence of the premier, the Silk and Miller families, and lots of media.

Joe asked his boss, Paul Sheridan, to clarify the reasons for his exclusion. Sheridan reluctantly explained that the decision was out of his hands. It had been made higher up.

Joe was devastated. So far, he'd been able to keep his pain and humiliation at work hidden from his parents. They were basking in the honour of having a son who'd not only worked hard and helped to catch the killers (with no small contribution from their unstinting support over four years of child care) but was now also the feted author of a best-selling book. How proud they were! But the awards event would be widely reported. How could he explain to his beloved parents that their son was being so dishonoured?

During this tense period, the bullying from his former colleagues made it clear that Joe had crossed the line. He was bombarded by abusive emails at work. It got to the point where every time he opened his inbox, he'd find something like this:

> *You are nothing short of a disgrace. You are a poor excuse for a copper. And even less of a human being. You profit from their deaths. You tell stories out of school. You tell crooks how we catch them. You have betrayed us.*

Joe was in no doubt about who had sent these emails, as the authors' Vicpol email addresses were at the top. His anxiety levels rocketed and his confidence plummeted. It took all his strength to go to work each day. Although he was getting strong support from many colleagues, the nasty behaviour he was facing confirmed his early suspicions that a few disgruntled members were agitating the rest.

Joe discussed this with Detective Inspector John Nolan, the ESD investigator. Nolan initially told him that the investigation had been instigated by 'a few hotheads from the Homicide Squad'.

Later, I asked Inspector Nolan about this. He said he was not at liberty to discuss what he'd said to Joe, but the sessions were taped so, if it was on tape, he must have said it. He went on to say that the investigation was initiated at a much higher level than 'a few hotheads'. I already knew that. Someone higher up had to approve the massive budget and expenditure of police time on what was rapidly becoming a far-reaching investigation involving a breach of the Police Regulations Act, which has no provisions for criminal offences or jail penalties.

Apparently without checking the Act, Channel 9 ran an evening bulletin on 16 June, using old footage of Joe leaving the Magistrates' Court to accompany a story claiming that he was at risk of being jailed for breach of police regulations. He was dismayed to discover that the police media unit had provided some of the material to Channel 9 and was astounded to realise that incorrect information about a possible jail term had been aired, yet the media unit hadn't corrected the reporter or contacted him to alert him to the story. The effect on his friends and family, especially his children, who all saw the item in peak viewing time, was gut-wrenching.

Still hoping to get onto the Government House list, Joe went higher up, to Commander Purton, Assistant Commissioner Overland and eventually Deputy Commissioner Kelly. He told them he'd done the Lorimer hard yards. So had his family. His marriage had ended. His kids were without a full-time mother. His own mother had taken on her grandchildren full time. Didn't his family deserve the recognition bestowed by such an award?

He received written advice from Commander Purton that he was not included because of the ESD investigation currently taking place. He pressed the issue further, pointing out that the ESD investigation significantly post-dated his Lorimer work. Before his book was released, his dedication and diligence had been recognised by his promotion to Acting Sergeant in the Fraud Squad. But now he was told that the decision was final and was 'based on departmental policy and long-standing practices'.

Unwilling to let it alone, Joe searched for relevant departmental policies, but he could find nothing. Repeated requests to his superior officers to provide him with the relevant 'long-standing practices' went unanswered. He could only assume that some other unrelated reason was the cause of the denial.

He was right.

In essence, the issue was how to manage disgruntled police and secure positive media coverage from the high-profile event. High-level discussions had been held on what to do about D'Alo. The atmosphere was still volatile. Decision-makers quaked at the thought that one little spark from the assembly at Government House – a shove, a dirty look, a snide remark – might lead to a scuffle or a sudden outbreak of violence in the ranks in front of the governor, the premier and the media. There was also a risk that the Silk and Miller families would be upset, might not even come, and might say something to the media. There was even a faint chance that some of the task force members would boycott the event and leak the reason to the media.

In the end, it was basically agreed that D'Alo had made himself and his family expendable and that his omission was a reasonable price to pay to secure the smooth and positive staging of the event. I probably would have endorsed the decision if I'd been responsible for police PR.

There was, however, another option. If police command simply wanted to prevent potential embarrassment at Government House, the Commissioner's Commendation Award could have been given to Joe at an alternate ceremony in another location. But the punishment was not only to exclude Joe from receiving the award in the presence of his family and mates, but to deny him the award altogether.

Pushed to the limit, Joe decided on 1 July 2003 to lodge his own complaint to ESD, but by 17 July he'd withdrawn the complaint, unwilling to prolong the ESD process any further.

The Government House event – one that could never be replicated – came and went. On that day, alone at his office, Joe was almost overcome by his sense of disappointment and exclusion. He felt that his unstinting efforts over the four years of the Lorimer Taskforce had been completely disregarded. The award, which symbolised recognition for dedication and diligence, had been withheld, defying natural justice.

On the home front, Joe was too ashamed to tell his family. He was relieved that his parents seemed to have missed the publicity. But then in October, his regular home-delivered issue of *Police Life* headlined the story with a group photo of everyone but Joe.

His parents were shocked and saddened. When Joe finally brought himself to read the article, he couldn't help focusing on the following passage, which mirrored the issues he'd constantly raised with command about his exclusion:

> *While this ceremony could never replace what people have sacrificed, it does recognise what they went through and that they should take heart from the positive results ... The ceremony was not only to recognise the people who had worked long and hard, but to acknowledge their families, partners, sons and daughters and friends who had also sacrificed a great deal to help us get the result in court.*

◆ ◆ ◆

Meanwhile, back at the ranch, things were getting worse. The ESD investigation into Joe's alleged infraction rumbled along. Eventually, three or four investigators worked on it for twelve months. More or less by osmosis, Joe discovered they were investigating whether he was in breach of Section 127A (1) of the Police Regulations Act.

This breach isn't serious enough to be grounds for termination of service. According to lawyers Tony Hargreaves and Andrew McKenna, the section is invoked all the time on trivial breaches, and the cases are usually heard in the Magistrates' Court.

Joe contended that all the information in his book was already in the public arena as a result of the trial, but ESD investigators said he must have been talking to Astle long before the trial, because the book was so far advanced by the time of the verdicts. This implied he *had* shared material with an outsider, which is what that section of the Act was intended to bar.

Joe countered by pointing to the release of another book on the subject, accompanied by a CD containing material that had not been heard by a jury. He also told them that the book *Underbelly 3*, written by two senior *Age* journalists, had been released in 1999 during the Lorimer investigation. He reminded ESD investigators that the *Underbelly* story compromised witnesses who later gave evidence at the Debs and Roberts trial. (Sheridan gave extensive evidence about this incident in court.) During the investigation, Joe said, a senior officer had personally told him to give one of the journalists, John Sylvester, access to the task force's files in the Lorimer office, which he believed resulted in a front-page story in the *Age*. (This was also discussed at length later in court.) But ESD was only interested in D'Alo. The other writers were not serving police officers.

Joe was also told that ESD's diligent investigations had revealed that he was in contempt of a court order because he'd disclosed the name of an informer whose identity was protected. This came as a shock to Joe, who was completely unaware of the order. The order had never come up previously, although the manuscript and book had been read by solicitor Mr Gibson, DPP Jeremy Rapke QC, Simon Overland, Old Uncle Tom Cobley and all. The contempt of court allegation never got a run in any court.

Concerned about the direction the ESD investigation was taking, Joe sought and obtained legal advice about his interview at the ESD office. The investigation seemed far too serious for a Police Regs breach. The next time he arrived at ESD, Inspector Nolan gave Joe a ten-page interview plan, which he was advised to read so he could familiarise himself with the direction of the questioning. Nolan left the room for a few minutes. When he sat down opposite Joe again, beside Senior Sergeant Long (it was a very top-heavy team to interview a Senior Constable), Joe said he was invoking his right to make a 'No Comment' interview.

Inspector Nolan seemed surprised, as Joe had indicated that he was willing to co-operate before obtaining legal advice. The officers left Joe alone in the room for the next forty minutes, then Nolan returned with an additional forty-two pages of interview.

Inspector Nolan later told me that the investigation was not that complicated. 'This was an obvious extended breach of 127A over a long period of time. Just a paperwork investigation, really. A one-off might be understood, but …'

So were they investigating Joe for each individual published page?

Joe's home life was also under siege. He had a new partner, but she'd recently been humiliated along with Joe at an official police function. She was trying to cope and support Joe, who now had a pre-teen daughter and a young son. The pressure being put on Joe reverberated through his family yet again. Joe and his partner were convinced their home was bugged and under surveillance. Their paranoid feelings seemed to be confirmed when his partner saw cars parked so they could scan the house in their otherwise quiet, leafy suburban street.

ESD investigators also raided Hardie Grant's offices with a search warrant, looking for any Victoria Police material that might have been used in the preparation of the book. Sandy Grant says he'd never been raided before (although later he had another visit from police before the publication of former high-flying solicitor Andrew Fraser's book *Court in the Middle*). Surprisingly, neither D'Alo's nor Astle's homes attracted the same attention.

Joe's partner was overcome by what was going on in their lives. Eventually, the strain became too much and they mutually agreed to part. Joe returned to his single-parent role while trying to be an active member of the police force.

He received great support from his immediate superiors, sometimes to their detriment, for which he is deeply grateful. But his determination to fight was becoming exhausting. In March 2004, ten months after the book's release, he took some unpaid leave. He felt unable to continue contributing effectively until the ESD investigation was concluded.

◆ ◆ ◆

Around this time, Hardie Grant decided to release an updated version of *One Down, One Missing,* including a new section about Jason Ghiller, Bandali Debs's original junior sidekick, who had taken part in a string of armed robberies. Joe and his colleagues had investigated these robberies as part of police Operation Hamada, then followed them up in the Armed Robbery squad, where Joe worked before he was moved to Lorimer. Joe was one of four Hamada investigators seconded to Lorimer because of his detailed knowledge of these robberies and the possible connection to the Moorabbin killings.

Jason Ghiller was Debs's nephew. At his court appearance, he pleaded guilty to a long string of offences over the previous eleven years: thirteen counts of armed robbery, three counts of recklessly causing serious injury, one count of intentionally causing serious injury, two counts of reckless conduct endangering life, one count of arson, one count of obtaining property by deception and one of aggravated burglary. For this impressive CV he only got ten years, with a six-year minimum.

He had told police that, during one robbery he'd done with Debs, Debs had shot a newsagent in the back, leaving him paralysed. When making his admissions, Ghiller had referred to the crippled man as 'the wheelchair cunt'. Debs couldn't be charged, because charging him would have identified the source as Ghiller, who had made several admissions to undercover police. Ghiller wasn't involved in the police murders, but he was investigated by the Lorimer Taskforce. Joe had included the story of this investigation in his original manuscript, but it had been withheld at the time because Ghiller was awaiting trial.

Joe told me later, 'Ghiller gave nothing away during his interview – essentially gave a "no comment" response to all questions. Most of the evidence against him was gathered during his time with our undercover police officer, when every meeting was being tape recorded.' Joe said that listening to those tapes was 'a great feeling', because he could tick off the armed Operation Pigout robberies on their list one by one. Joe said, 'This cemented the evidence not only against Ghiller, but Debs as well, even though Debs wasn't committed for trial on any of the older robberies.'

Ghiller's guilty plea on 23 September 2003 opened the door for a new, improved edition of *One Down, One Missing* to replace the one that had been recalled and pulped. After the recall, there had been some discussion between Joe, Astle and the publisher about producing a second edition at some future time, but Joe had no current knowledge of the state of play. In fact, Hardie Grant had decided to republish and had sent a letter to police command along with the new manuscript, advising them that 'in good faith' they wanted to 'iron out any issues' prior to publication.

There was no response or acknowledgement, so Hardie Grant again wrote to police command and the legal adviser's office requesting a response. They advised that if there was no response, republication would proceed, including new chapters, and with informer names and identities changed or protected. The publisher also phoned but received no response or action.

On 30 July 2004, out of the blue, Joe received a direction not to permit the publication of the new edition, of which he had no prior knowledge. If he didn't stop it, the direction stated, he would be charged with more disciplinary offences. He'd already been charged by ESD for allegedly breaching Section 127A of the Police Regulation Act and was in discussions with his lawyer, Tony Hargreaves, preparing for a contested hearing at the Magistrates' Court, so he contacted Hargreaves and informed him of the unfolding situation.

Hargreaves wrote to Assistant Commissioner Walshe at ESD and explained that the contractual agreement with the publishers meant that Joe was unable to stop publication. To emphasise his point, Hargreaves provided Walshe with a copy of the Hardie Grant letter. Walshe was unmoved by the information and reaffirmed the direction.

Hargreaves asked Walshe to identify what preventative steps could be taken, given that the publisher had enforced his right to publish. Hargreaves also suggested that if the concerns of Victoria Police were so significant, then the Chief Commissioner should contact the publisher explaining the legal concerns barring the book's release. Walshe responded that 'it was not a matter for the force'. He said that the obviously illogical direction should be complied with, again hitting the ball back over the net to D'Alo.

In early December 2004, the sanitised but still unsanctioned version of *One Down, One Missing* was released in time for Christmas. Joe's festive season that year was not very merry. On 12 January 2005 he was informed that ESD wanted him to return for another chat the following day. On Joe's behalf, Hargreaves asked how his client could have prevented publication and was told that there were several possibilities, one being for Joe to issue an injunction. When Hargreaves inquired why Victoria Police hadn't done this themselves, he was told the force did not want to wear the legal costs – they were Joe's responsibility.

When I heard this later, it seemed to me that the cost to Vicpol of an injunction was a mere bagatelle in view of the money already spent on investigating Joe's regulation breaches. An injunction would also have saved them the much greater costs of many subsequent personnel hours and court appearances. I tried to contact police command, making four phone calls and sending three emails via the media unit to see if I could ask them myself. But when I tried to speak to Deputy Commissioner Simon Overland, Assistant Commissioner Steve Fontana and Commander Terry Purton, the response was that 'unfortunately the people you are wishing to speak to will be unavailable to facilitate your request'. It seemed the book was still attracting legal interest, and this was one of those times when 'no' meant 'no'.

◆ ◆ ◆

The Magistrates' Court appearance was set down for Monday 7 February 2005. Hargreaves had briefed Andrew McKenna, a very experienced barrister. On the preceding Friday, Joe received a call from McKenna, indicating that he needed an urgent meeting. Joe and Rob O'Neill from Tony Hargreaves' office met with McKenna from 4 pm until midnight that Friday, discussing the contents of six thick folders. (This was a case of bombarding the opposition with paperwork!) They reconvened for another long meeting on the Sunday.

On arrival at court, Joe was tense. He had always stood on the police side of the courtroom and felt very nervous about being on the wrong side. The police paperwork was voluminous. Plan A was to fight it out, but after McKenna conferred with the Vicpol lawyers he came back and set out the options for Plan B. His expression was grim. There had been up to thirteen charges of breaching Section 127A, but the team had whittled them down to six or seven. The offer was that if Joe pleaded guilty, he would only be charged with one count. He'd cop the fine and McKenna would argue against a conviction.

McKenna was very charming and helpful when I spoke to him later. 'Once we knew the other side's position, our view was that our position was untenable owing to the nature of the material he had exposed,' McKenna said. 'His duty required him not to disclose that information. I suppose, in mitigation, I don't think he really appreciated the sensitivity. He seemed to think because it had been submitted to Gibson and Rapke, he was in the clear. Even in the courtroom, I think he honestly believed that. But he'd let out names of certain sources … We hoped to avoid a conviction, but we were not successful.' McKenna told me he often defends police charged with breaches of Section 127A. They're usually trivial breaches, like helping out a civilian mate with some low-level information.

Joe had to make a momentous decision quickly. He understood that if he pleaded not guilty, the Crown would trot out more revelations of confidential information, which would compound his mistake. Wishing he was anywhere else in the world, he pleaded guilty, copped a fine of $1500 and had the conviction recorded. His shame was acute.

Later on, I asked Tony Hargreaves if he thought the resources spent on convicting a cop with a previously blameless record and several commendations was a good investment of taxpayers' funds. 'There is no doubt that the police will spend unlimited funds on prosecuting other police,' Hargreaves said. 'They have bottomless budgets, QCs, endless resources, all lined up against our firm, which represents a lot of police. I had a case once where a policeman shot a magpie, and they paid for *two* autopsies on the magpie!' He said that a good deal was negotiated for Joe D'Alo. 'We were not going to win.'

When I put Hargreaves' comments to Joe, he said, 'That's quite a surprise, because he was really pushing to contest the charges rather than plead guilty. His view at the time was that I personally was not the publisher and did not have the power to release the job. The publisher was Hardie Grant. Looking back, I wish I'd taken Hargreaves' advice, but I guess at the time I was so gutted by the process, I didn't have the energy or the spirit to keep fighting, so I made the decision to plead guilty.'

Joe was approached by another lawyer, who expressed dismay that Joe had pleaded guilty and outlined some arguments that Joe should advance to appeal his guilty plea and argue why he was not guilty as charged by the police. It sounded a lot like the original Plan A initially favoured by Hargreaves and McKenna. Joe decided to bite the bullet, to try to overturn his conviction. They lost in the County Court and then in the Supreme Court. Now Joe had a conviction, a fine *and* a big legal bill.

When a police officer is charged with an offence, he can apply to the Police Association to assist with legal fees. Sometimes these fees escalate into millions of dollars.

On the day Joe applied to the association, he sat waiting his turn to be heard alongside some well-connected police who had been charged with extremely serious offences. They got their funding, but he was knocked back. This meant he had to fight another battle with the heads of the association, some of whom he said were friends with the officers who had it in for him. He finally did get most of his fees paid by the association, but it was another argument he didn't need.

While Joe's court appearance and appeal were in train, he was asked to attend an interview at the Office of Police Integrity (OPI). An invitation to talk to the OPI comes with some serious conditions attached. You're not allowed to tell anyone, even your nearest and dearest. There are some exceptions: you can talk to a lawyer, speak to others to obtain necessary documents for the OPI, and if the threat of being absent for hours on end without explanation might place a strain on your relationship or health, the director might allow you to tell your partner that you're attending Victoria's equivalent of the Star Chamber. But anyone you tell has to be sworn to secrecy, and you can't tell them why you're there.

Rob Hudson MLA, the Labor member for Bentleigh in the Victorian House of Assembly, addressed parliament on the OPI's powers in September 2007. He said:

> *Let us have a look at what the Office of Police Integrity can do. Its director can hold hearings; summon witnesses to give*

evidence under oath and produce documents; obtain warrants to enter and search premises and seize documents and other things; and require a member of the police force to answer questions. When it is in the public interest the director can compel witnesses to provide information or to produce a document or thing which may incriminate a witness. It is not an excuse before the Office of Police Integrity to say, 'I might incriminate myself.' ... The Office of Police Integrity, the director and the chief examiner can force that officer to answer questions.

The OPI can also initiate investigations under its 'own motion' powers. It doesn't have to rely on a complaint or on proven police misconduct.

Joe D'Alo attended the OPI on 5 May 2005 to answer questions. He had no choice this time. 'No comment' was not an option. He still isn't allowed to say anything about what happened. He says he answered in a frank and forthright way. His lawyer, Phil Barravecchio, sat through these interviews with him.

The OPI in Victoria evolved in response to a growing police accountability crisis. For many years, there had been calls for a royal commission to inquire into Victoria Police. There had been allegations of corruption in the service under both Chief Commissioner Neil Comrie and his successor, Christine Nixon. The independent ombudsman's office was responsible for reviewing police complaints but was under-resourced for the task, and this created a very uncomfortable situation for the Victorian government.

In April 2004, attempting to silence the critics, the government established a separate police ombudsman's position with sweeping powers and gave him an extra $1m to help root out police corruption. But within eight weeks, the model was overhauled again. This time, the government announced that another $10m would be bestowed on the new office, which would also have phone-tapping powers. But the federal attorney-general intervened to invalidate those powers, arguing that they were excessive and unnecessary for an ombudsman's office. So, on 24 August 2004, four months after creating the office, the government abandoned the idea of a police ombudsman and established a new position of Director of Police Integrity in an Office of Police Integrity, in the hope that this new nomenclature would persuade the attorney-general to change his mind. The same person filled both offices, lawyer and career public servant George Brouwer.

The ombudsman's office and the OPI were said to be independent of each other, but it was a ludicrous proposition. When the same person was heading up both agencies, blind Freddie could see that the offices couldn't be autonomous. What was the director of the OPI to do if he obtained information that should properly be investigated by the ombudsman? Would he refer it to himself, then sprint across to his other office to change hats and deliberate? Or perhaps send himself an email? And who would respond? If Gilbert and Sullivan had been around, the OPI show would have been on at Her Majesty's Theatre.

Community organisations and the media had a go at watching the watchers. During 2004 and 2005, the OPI suffered quite a bit of bad press. On the ABC's *PM* program on 16 February 2005, Nick McKenzie of the *Age* reported that an anti-corruption detective who'd been seconded to the OPI the previous August had submitted an internal report detailing 'a number of failings in the OPI, including poor investigation procedures and instances of poor and ineffective management'.

Graham Ashton for the OPI responded defensively that the officer in question 'isn't the font of all knowledge in relation to the establishment of policy and procedures'. McKenzie reminded him that 'with calls for a royal commission still a very recent memory, evidence of the success of the OPI is crucial to the state government, and any perceptions of failure potentially incredibly damaging'. The detective who authored the critical report was rapped over the knuckles and moved to another unit.

Child psychologist Dr Reina Michaelson was another thorn in the OPI's side. In 1992, she claimed that Victoria Police members were protecting child abusers and even participating in abuse themselves. Four of the cases she raised were reviewed by the ombudsman's office, and the issue was then passed on to the new OPI.

In March 2005, Dr Michaelson was in the news again. She'd given the *Age* tapes of an interview with the OPI in which a senior investigator had told her the government had set up the OPI in order to have 'something that looks more like a crime commission', but that it lacked the power and resources to investigate corruption and organised crime. The investigator also told her that with limited resources, choices had to be made about which complaints against police were investigated.

When I read about the lack of resources, I wondered again about how much was spent on investigating Joe D'Alo's contravention of Police Regulation 127A.

I decided to phone Dr Michaelson and check the story. She was hard to find. After about a dozen phone calls, I concluded she'd either gone overseas or gone to ground. Her *Age* interview had sparked attempts to discredit her professionally and personally, and I wondered if they'd achieved their objective. But, in the end, my persistence achieved results.

She was both concerned and pleased when I located her. 'I am pleased it was difficult,' she said. 'After what I went through ...'

She told me that the ombudsman's report in 2004 had been damning. It found the four cases had been bungled and was highly critical of two senior detectives, who were named. She believes they weren't charged. And, despite her efforts, the report wasn't tabled in parliament.

The OPI was again the focus of unflattering media coverage in August 2005, when Melbourne media reported extensively and adversely that the OPI had accidentally dispatched more than 400 confidential police files to a member of the public. Defending the OPI in parliament, Police

Minister Tim Holding described the incident as 'regrettable'. The OPI director, George Brouwer, called it a 'clerical error'.

Both comments were astonishing understatements, considering the damage done to the privacy of the individuals involved and to the credibility of the OPI. Its investigation methods, its check-and-balance auditing and the accuracy of the information it provided were all in doubt, as was the model of the two supposedly separate departments. There were more calls for royal commissions and for a truly independent anti-corruption body that would not have the daily dilemma of investigating itself.

Ironically, it was against this background that the OPI director George Brouwer set out to investigate the circumstances surrounding the publication of Joe's book and the 'actions of Victoria Police in obtaining a copy of the manuscript, in evaluating its contents and subsequent attempts to prevent or delay publication'. By this time, the OPI really needed a win.

Mr Brouwer had undertaken the investigation on his 'own motion powers', which meant he'd initiated it himself, not at the request of anyone else. The new investigation represented a chance for the OPI to get some runs on the board, after the savaging it had received since its creation the previous year. The sacrifice of a single police officer in a case that had already been ruled on by a court could be of no concern to the OPI.

More broadly, Brouwer's investigation into Joe and the writing of *One Down, One Missing* assessed Victoria Police policies and practices on informer and information management at the time to 'determine the extent to which the Lorimer Taskforce and D'Alo had complied with these practices'. Finally, the inquiry assessed subsequent changes to police informer and information management policies to 'determine the likelihood of a similar occurrence in the future'. The investigation had extended over several months, involving several officers, a lot of resources and a bucket of money.

◆ ◆ ◆

On 15 September 2005, almost two years after Joe D'Alo's book was released, Brouwer presented a report to the Victorian parliament on issues to do with the book.

Brouwer's findings were damning, particularly in relation to Joe. The report described Joe as 'steadfast and obstinate' in his determination to disclose information about the Lorimer Taskforce's operations. The OPI director claimed that police attempts to gain access to the manuscript had been stymied until it was too late to permit 'considered and effective action'.

Brouwer recommended that there should be stiffer penalties for breaches of Section 127A, which was the section that had been invoked against Joe. At the time, the 'not more than 20 penalty units' would have translated into a maximum fine of $2000. Brouwer suggested that the fine be increased and a new, second-tier offence be created to cover the unauthorised disclosure of information 'with intent'.

Joe was amazed and angry when the director presented his report to parliament days before Joe's Supreme Court appeal. Joe considered the report at best a character assassination and believed it would probably have been actionable if it had been released outside parliament. Under parliamentary privilege, however, nothing that's written in a report to parliament can be prosecuted for defamation. In a letter to Mr Brouwer, which was never answered, Joe said, 'The report makes a number of defamatory comments and assumptions without providing evidence in support of the claims. It lacks credibility, independence and fairness by failing to include material I provided to your investigators.'

In his introduction, Brouwer says that 'the book disclosed sensitive operational methodologies used by Victoria Police'. Right! This made it like many books and news stories in the public arena, including my own. If the prospect of dying in jail is no deterrent to murder, a book that describes how the cops will hunt you down might do the trick.

Brouwer also observed instances where informers were identified by name (in the first edition) or by circumstances (in the second). This is correct. It is what made me think Joe D'Alo was going to cop it when I read the first book. How this got past the legal advisers is a mystery to me. Anyone with a working knowledge of defamation law would surely have got a nasty little jolt when those names and informer numbers hove into view. This was Joe D'Alo's (and the publisher's) big stuff-up. Ignorance of Section 127A was no excuse.

At the time of publication, Joe had little knowledge of defamation law either. Reliance on people more experienced in the non-fiction publishing process was partly to blame for Joe's failure to change names and think through the potential risks. He says, 'Over 250 characters were named in the book. Many of these were criminals, who'd had their day in court and in most cases they were convicted. They were not secret spies that only a select number of Lorimer knew. Most had their names mentioned during the Debs/Roberts trial. They were only mentioned in relation to Lorimer, not in detail in other respects – no different than other true crime books, whose writers got their inside information from an insider. In hindsight, though, I agree that pseudonyms should have been used. Both Astle and I discussed this on several occasions with the publisher.'

Brouwer also claimed that 'Victoria Police made a concerted effort to obtain a copy of the MS prior to its publication once the A/C (Crime) became aware of its existence'. Brouwer says Overland 'was thwarted by D'Alo in his efforts … and effective action became almost impossible'. A senior constable thwarting Assistant Commissioner Overland, a man with a first-class honours degree in law? The full force of Victoria Police impotent to act? Could he be serious? Senior police were offered several opportunities to read the manuscript prior to publication. They could also have taken out injunctions for both editions, but they chose not to do so.

The introduction goes on to say 'it was unfortunate that Victoria Police was not able to advise affected parties of the pending publication, largely due to the delay in receiving the MS'. Wrong! It is documented that the manuscript was available (under conditions) to Mr Overland several days before publication, and he'd known about it for six weeks. He had a big staff, a lot of clout and numerous telephones at his disposal. Why not give the publisher a call? Or get one of his minions to read it?

Brouwer continues, 'I have not found any evidence that D'Alo did not comply with the informer and information management practices applying at the time. His access to information during the investigation was authorised and justified.' Well, that was something of a concession. But then he went on, 'I have, however, *drawn the conclusion,* [my italics] that he inappropriately accessed the Law Enforcement Assistance Program (LEAP) after the investigations, to obtain details for the book.'

What were the grounds for this conclusion? Joe admitted accessing the LEAP a few times after the arrest of Debs and Roberts. He knew his access would be recorded. When asked almost three years later about three specific occasions when he'd had access, he said he couldn't recall the details but thought he may have been accessing the information in case he was required to give evidence at the trial. Or maybe for some other reason. LEAP access was part of his daily activities when he checked on known criminals in his new Fraud Squad appointment. Just as when you follow a Google trail, often one suspect's details would lead to known associates, and so on through the system. Brouwer didn't believe this.

Brouwer also claimed that Joe could have provided the manuscript to Victoria Police at any time. This is misleading, to say the least. Vicpol were in possession of several legal opinions saying that he was *not* in a position to do this.

Joe's position was misrepresented to parliament, with no right of reply. In the body of the report, Mr Brouwer recognised that Joe 'had full and authorised access to all material gathered during the … investigation', but he didn't seem to realise that checking details in a book would require many more than three hits, though these were the only ones recorded. That three LEAP hits would be enough to check more than 250 characters named in the book is stretching credulity. His report appears to indicate that Joe was being less than truthful about his use of LEAP. D'Alo vehemently denied this at interview and continues to do so.

My main problem with Mr Brouwer's report is that it seemed to be politically expedient to hang D'Alo out to dry to enable an upgrade of police regulations and justify the emotive language and long bows drawn from Brouwer's 'conclusions' and opinions. Many of these were not supported by facts or were denied by D'Alo. Only one of his denials got a mention, and even that was not believed.

These inquiries are held behind closed doors, in secrecy, with the person under investigation not allowed to let anyone know that he is being investigated and what is happening. More like the Spanish Inquisition, where the investigator is also the judge. In a normal inquiry, the defendant has the right to a defence.

Here are a few of the emotive words used to describe Joe D'Alo and his actions, pulled at random from the report. He is variously described as 'steadfast and obstinate', displaying 'obduracy', 'secretiveness and delays' and 'unable to provide a reasonable explanation'. He had 'mistakenly or deliberately misled' others; he had 'wilfully delayed' police access to the manuscript; he was repeatedly described as having 'misused' information and as having 'accessed LEAP inappropriately'. Brouwer commented unfavourably on his 'determination to proceed' 'for his own benefit'; and it goes on.

Joe now says, 'I am confident if I'd had the right to defend the accusations, the outcome would have been different. In retrospect, this is what really bugs me – the unfairness of not being allowed to be heard in my own defence.'

Mr Brouwer declined to speak to me for this story. He deputised Inspector John Nolan, the officer who had previously investigated Joe at ESD and was now at OPI. Nolan didn't write the report and was unable to answer the questions I most wanted to ask the director, particularly about his subjective use of language. He undertook to take the questions to Mr Brouwer, but I didn't expect an answer, despite Mr Nolan's friendly tone. He told me, 'The director doesn't want to discuss operational matters.'

The core issue in the report is Brouwer's statement that 'despite D'Alo's protestations to the contrary, I am not persuaded that he was ignorant of his obligations to Victoria Police and the potential consequences of his actions.'

A key objective of the investigation and report was Brouwer's recommendation about the offence and penalty provisions of Section 127A, which he said should be amended to provide for a maximum two years' imprisonment for unauthorised release of information and/or a substantial fine. He also said the amendment should include a 'with intent' provision with a maximum penalty of up to ten years.

◆ ◆ ◆

In October 2007, a Victorian government press release announced that the Brumby government had provided $51.1 million to the OPI, which now had a staff of 100 people. It also announced that the OPI had 'questioned 68 people using its coercive questioning powers' and recommended changes to Victoria Police practices 'to reduce opportunities for corruption'.

I couldn't help thinking that seemed like quite a lot of public funding to facilitate the questioning of sixty-eight people. Joe was one of those people. Judging from the money and resources spent on a relatively trivial regulations breach, how far did the rest of the budget extend to investigating serious allegations, like Dr Michaelson's naming of police officers involved in pornography and paedophilia?

Possibly the only positive outcome from this sad saga was that in 2003, after the book's publication, Victoria Police overhauled the way informers' identities were managed internally, creating a separate and secure informer management unit along with new reporting and audit regimes.

Joe D'Alo resigned from Victoria Police on 9 February 2007.

On 1 April 2007 the Police Regulations Act was amended to include new penalties for breaches of regulation 127A. The penalty of 20 units is now a penalty of 240 units, two years' imprisonment or both. More-serious breaches attract the sanction of 600 units, five years' imprisonment or both. Expect fewer books from police insiders. Helping a mate out might no longer be an option, and as for those media leaks …

On 12 March 2008, Joe was told by the Police Association that all the police officers who attended the scene of the Silk and Miller murders were being granted an *ex gratia* payment to compensate for not receiving grief counselling or assistance with post-traumatic stress disorder, but he'd been omitted. The amount was not great, but the impact of being punished yet again was a final punch in the guts.

◆ ◆ ◆

Some who read this story may enjoy the fact that Joe D'Alo paid such a high personal and professional price for his transgressions. A few may think he deserved it. Others may feel that he should have been more careful in considering the ramifications of his ultimately disastrous project.

And those who supported him will feel sad that such overwhelming resources were used to crush one man who crossed the line.

Regardless of feelings, the facts are that in the course of writing a widely acclaimed, best-selling book, D'Alo did breach Section 127A of Police Regulations, although he did so with good intentions. He was found guilty in a properly convened court and failed in two appeals. He now has a conviction recorded against his name.

He has never received a cent from the book.

Using names of registered informers and others was ill-considered and possibly dangerous to the informers. In mitigation, Joe only left the names in because he accepted the reassurance of other, more-experienced people that the manuscript was publishable.

Some members of Victoria Police behaved towards Joe in an unprofessional and bullying manner. As he twisted and squirmed under the inexorable weight of the system, some might argue that the punishment was disproportionate to the offence.

The OPI investigation was overkill, finding nothing more about D'Alo than the court had found already, and the timing was politically expedient.

Some of the police I have been able to speak to express regret for the way things turned out, but still find it difficult to forgive Joe the writer. Others – including some well-known, well-respected police officers – have already expressed admiration for him in dozens of emails. One advised him, 'Don't worry about all the commotion. Ride out the stormy seas, as they will eventually become calm again. You have my support.' Another wrote, 'I hope that you stand tall, remain proud and deal with this adversity with the same professionalism and poise that enabled you to contribute to the solving of the murder of our two colleagues.' There are many more.

After Joe resigned, a senior officer wrote to him, apologising for the way he'd been treated by Vicpol and 'hoping the treatment had not been motivated by malice, simply a poor judgement call'. Another member expressed reservations about the matters he'd described, saying, 'I would hope that investigative techniques and the darker side of the politics would not be shown to the public.'

Joe has moved on. He has made a new life as a highly regarded builder and home designer, specialising in the use of sustainable materials and incorporating some refinements of his own invention. He now has a loving partner, his devoted family and staunch friends alongside him. He recently became a proud grandfather. Police and many others recognise his book as inspiring.

Joe D'Alo said in a letter to then Chief Commissioner Christine Nixon, 'Perhaps it's a pity that my career ended this way. Or perhaps I was merely a number, easily discarded and easily replaced?'

Whatever you think, the costs and collateral damage were overwhelming and ongoing. The moral of the story might be that you cross the police line at your peril. None of Joe's investigative work has been questioned.

Postscript

Jason Roberts had been protesting his innocence ever since he was imprisoned, and he managed to persuade Detective Senior Sergeant Ron Iddles to review his conviction. Iddles shed doubt on Roberts' conviction in a report to police command, which was picked up by the *Herald Sun* and turned into a media campaign. The ensuing inquiry uncovered a slip-up in police procedure during the Lorimer investigation that would provide enough evidence for Roberts to get a retrial.

In 2015, the Independent Broad-based Anti-corruption Commission (IBAC) enquired into Victoria Police conduct concerning Operation Lorimer. The inquiry focused on the statements of the police who were first responders to the murder scene, particularly those who comforted and spoke to Miller before his transport to hospital and his subsequent death. This inquiry found there was no conclusive evidence to substantiate allegations of improper conduct in the recording of statements and, in February 2016, the IBAC inquiry was concluded.

But that was not the end of it. Anthony Dowsley, an intrepid *Herald Sun* journalist, had been digging around for evidence of cases where police had doctored statements. In one of the piles of paperwork he'd obtained during his project, he came across a copy of the original statement made by Senior Constable Glenn Pullin, who was one of the last people to speak with Miller before his death.

Pullin's first statement had been destroyed, then rewritten and backdated, but a carbon copy had survived in the archives. In the statement used at Roberts' trial, Pullin was talking to Senior Constable Miller:

> I said to him, 'Did you hit him?' He replied, 'I don't think so.'
> [My emphasis.]

Then came a new part:

> *I also asked him, 'Were* they *in a car or on foot?' And he replied*
> they *were on foot. I asked him, 'How long ago did that happen?'*
> *He replied, 'A couple of minutes.'*

Normally, this would have been classed as hearsay, but it was admissible because it was part of a dying declaration. But it seems that when Glenn Pullin, a junior officer who had been shattered by his experience, made his original statement about Rod Miller's dying words, he didn't say 'they' but 'he'. Much later, it emerged that his statement had been rewritten at the behest of a senior Homicide officer, Detective Sergeant George Buckhorn, to indicate that there were two offenders.

The usual procedure for making statements to police is that if you make a statement on, say, 10 March, then remember something more in April, you can make another statement starting with words like, 'I have previously made a statement about this matter ...' then set out the new material in a supplementary statement. The big issue in this case was that Pullin's alleged recollection of Miller's dying words was *retrospectively* inserted into the contemporaneous original statement, which then appeared under *the old date*. During Roberts' trial, the revised statement was used to indicate that there was more than one offender. Jason Roberts has always denied he was there.

Realising the explosive nature of his find, Dowsley handed the copy to Detective Senior Sergeant Ron Iddles in November 2017. Iddles and Detective Senior Sergeant Bezzina took the information to IBAC. Pullin had previously told IBAC he couldn't recall whether he'd made a second statement, but it could now be shown that the trial brief in Debs' and Roberts' prosecution contained a statement by Pullin that was substantially different in detail from the original.

As a result of this new evidence, the investigation was reopened, and on 10 November 2020, Jason Roberts had his convictions quashed by Victoria's highest court. Roberts had spent more than half his life in prison for the murders of two Victorian police officers, but the court found there had been a miscarriage of justice and ordered a new trial. Unfortunately, the error by Pullin and Buckhorn had tarnished the rest of the evidence collected over more than four years.

Joe says that he is confident the evidence against Roberts remains solid. 'There is the listening device evidence, his close connection to the Hyundai, his attempts to repair the screen, and further tactical evidence.' He believes this has much more weight than a single administrative error.

Ballistics testing on the bullets recovered from the bodies of Silk and Miller revealed that two different firearms were used in the murders. Silk was shot in the guts through the passenger window of the Hyundai, then later executed by a close-range shot to his head as he lay injured on the ground. A different gun fired the fatal shots at Miller through the back window of the car. Unless the killer was Billy the Kid, it's obvious there were two shooters.

There is widening fallout. Buckhorn and Pullin have left the job and now both work in unrelated industries – years of training gone to waste. Chief Commissioner Simon Overland resigned on 16 June 2011 after critics placed him under intense public pressure over failings in the management of a police computer system, which didn't alert front-line officers to the parole status of the people they interacted with. As a result, parolees went on to kill six people.

Overland has subsequently worked in various administrative positions outside the police. He was summoned to appear at the Royal Commission into the Management of Police Informants to answer questions about his knowledge of running barrister turned police informer Nicola Gobbo, which is a whole new story!

He gave evidence that he didn't recall anything about Gobbo acting as a police informant during his term as commissioner, but his long-lost police diaries, providentially discovered in a police basement document storage, indicated differently. Royal commissioner Margaret McMurdo AC sighed at one point that the process of investigating police was akin to 'a magical mystery tour'. She also commented that 'when those whom the community entrusts to uphold and enforce the law breach fundamental legal obligations, confidence in our justice system and indeed our democracy, is seriously diminished.' She got that right! As a result of the royal commission, Simon Overland now awaits further investigation into his role in the Gobbo debacle.

After Roberts was granted a retrial, the families of Silk and Miller released a statement saying they were 'devastated' by the court's decision.

'It is not the decision we were hoping to hear, 22 long years after Gary and Rod were murdered,' they said. 'A number of lives changed when Gary and Rod were murdered, and lives will never be the same.'

Joe D'Alo's life was one of them.

Further reading

One Down, One Missing by Joe D'Alo and David Astle.

IBAC report on proceedings, 4 February 2019 <https://ibac.vic. gov.au/docs/default-source/operation-gloucester/transcripts/ ibac-operation-gloucester-day-1-transcript---4-february-2019. pdf?sfvrsn=84981729_6>

Lawyer X by Anthony Dowsley and Patrick Carlyon (HarperCollins, 2020).

Chapter Two

KISSING TOADS

My Nanna had a saying, 'Before you meet your handsome prince, you'll have to kiss a lot of toads.' But what if your handsome prince is someone others would consider a toad? Over the years, I've spoken with many women in this situation, including a lot of prison WAGs (wives and girlfriends). Some journalists call them crimbos, implying that they're airheads. In fact, many of these women are intelligent and attractive; they're just drawn to men who live in the fast lane.

In every prison, there are people serving long sentences who have partners on the outside. They try to keep their relationships going with phone calls, letters and periodic prison visits. In non-contact visits, a bulletproof glass screen separates prisoners from visitors, and the women are known as 'glass widows'. Some relationships are kept going by lies. The prisoner wants to believe the partner is faithful, and the partner is unlikely to disabuse them of the notion, which is where the lies come in.

When men are sent to prison, some instruct their women to forget them, get a divorce, never visit, make a new life. Others get 'mail' from a friend on the phone that the missus is playing up. This news can lead to rages and smashed prison phones, leaving all the other inmates to go without one more thing until the lines are restored.

Women too have partners who remain staunch, mind the kids and keep the home fires burning until the partner's release, sometimes even when the partner is serving time for attempting to murder them! But women generally serve shorter sentences than men, because their crimes tend to be smart and tricky rather than violent or deadly, so there are fewer male partners 'doing life' on the outside than women.

One incredibly staunch girlfriend is the woman who loves Keith Faure, a career criminal who is serving twenty-four years and a concurrent life sentence of nineteen years without parole, which means he'll get out in 2025 when he's seventy-four, if he lives that long. Faure's convictions include four armed robberies, two manslaughter convictions and one break and enter. He has been tried for five murders and convicted of two. He has also 'rolled over' and helped police with their inquiries on several gangland killings in Melbourne. He's spent most of his adult life in prison.

One day, I received a call from his partner, Jenny*, asking me to visit him with her. He was already in maximum security after conviction for one murder. Other matters were still to be heard, so his safety was of paramount importance to the police. He wanted to see if I'd be interested in writing a history of his family.

His family is a crime dynasty going back three generations. His grandfather, Norm Bruhn, was active in the Sydney underworld in the 1920s. Bruhn was shot and killed in 1927 during a hit ordered by Snowy Cutmore, who himself died four months later along with Squizzy Taylor in a Melbourne shoot-out. Faure's dad was a notorious painter and docker in the 1960s and '70s who took his entire family on the run and lived 'in smoke' under an assumed name for fifteen years. His mother, who stood by all her criminal men, was at a party one night when the head of a man beside her exploded all over her party dress. He'd been shot as a payback for something or other.

Keith's younger brother, Les, was doing fourteen years down the hall from Keith for murdering his girlfriend in 1997. Their youngest brother, Noel, was convicted of manslaughter for a killing in 1990. On 19 May 2004, he was rearrested with Keith in relation to the Melbourne gangland killing of Lewis Moran, another murderer. Noel received a life sentence for his part in the Moran execution, but died not far into it.

Moran had been gunned down when masked gunmen entered the Brunswick Club on Sydney Road in Brunswick at approximately 6.40 pm on 31 March 2004. Moran must have figured they were after him, because he left the bar and ran through a poker-machine room before the gunman caught up with him and shot him twice, the fatal bullet being fired into the back of his head from a few centimetres away.

Caine's drinking mate, Bertie Wrout, was severely wounded by a second gunman who was guarding the door, but he survived the attack.

No prizes for guessing who the second gunman was. Gangland boss Tony Mokbel paid Evangelos Goussis and his mate Keith Faure $140,000 for the murder, but it wasn't long before the police tracked them down. When they were put on trial for murder, Keith rolled over in return for a pile of inducements, including monthly contact visits with Jenny, he told me. He became a prosecution witness with a number instead of a name. This was quite ridiculous, because everyone knew it was him, singing like a canary to load up his mate. For his cooperation, Keith escaped doing any further time.

On Keith's evidence, Goussis was found guilty of the murder of Lewis Moran and sentenced to life with a minimum of thirty years without parole. But in 2013, rumblings emerged in various quarters about the nature of the evidence used to secure Goussis's convictions. It was claimed that contradictory accounts by the primary prosecution witness (which was Keith) had been rewritten to fit with telephone-call records provided to the court by police. In 2014, Goussis released his own account of events, alleging police misconduct, and called for a royal commission.

Keith retaliated by implicating Goussis and himself in the murder of Shane Chartes-Abbott, another unsolved gangland murder, but on 8 July 2014 a Victorian Supreme Court jury found Goussis and his two co-accused not guilty of that murder. (The murder of Chartes-Abbott is still unsolved, although no-one is racing to take the investigation further.)

Keith had been arrested quite recently when Jenny conveyed his invitation to me. I'm always curious to meet prisoners' wives and girlfriends, so I agreed to meet her in the car park at Barwon Prison near Geelong.

I found her to be a pleasant, quite well-educated woman in her forties. She was living near the prison to be near Keith. She had spent nearly ten years with him when he was out of prison, and they lived together very happily, she told me. She thought he'd finally gone straight, but then he started behaving furtively, and she began to suspect that his old connections were again leading him astray.

Sure enough, she was with Keith and Noel, shopping in the Bay City Plaza, when about twelve Special Operations Group cops pounced and wrestled Keith and Noel to the ground. Cars full of detectives pulled up soon after. 'They arrested me too,' she told me as we walked towards the forbidding prison gates.

Her dreams of living a normal life with Keith, making plans together for their future, were dashed that day. Her contact with him after his arrest was a weekly non-contact visit, sitting opposite him in a smelly little cubicle with a twenty-millimetre sheet of bulletproof glass between them and an armed warder standing behind Keith, who was in a similar cubicle. A small mike in the glass relayed their sweet nothings to each other, and everything was recorded. Visits lasted about forty-five minutes once a week. For nineteen years …

'I'll wait for him,' Jenny told me after we left. 'He's a wonderful man really. He just got in with the wrong people.' And the money was good, I didn't say. The going rate for gangland hits was around $150,000 each.

Keith did wrangle a marginally better spot in prison as part of his rollover deal, but when I next visited, he was still in protection, which is where the authorities keep the 'dogs' (police informers) and 'rock spiders' (paedophiles). The visit was in a library, across a table, with a hatchet-faced guard watching us unblinkingly to prevent the passing of contraband, or even touching.

Keith told me that at any one time he was only allowed to be in the company of two other prisoners he trusted, whom he could nominate. Which was no protection at all for some dogs, as Carl Williams discovered on 19 April 2010, when a 'trusted' cellmate bashed him to death.

In spite of Keith Faure's gruesome reputation, I found him entertaining and charming, but, after two visits, I decided against writing his family history. My husband mentioned that he probably still had associates on the outside, and they might worry about what he was telling me. 'I don't want you to walk out one day into the end of a rifle,' he said convincingly.

◆ ◆ ◆

Another glamorous and very public girlfriend was Zarah Garde-Wilson, a solicitor with killer heels and killer clients who acted for many of the infamous individuals involved in the Melbourne underworld. Gangland victim Lewis Caine was her partner at the time of his murder. They had been a couple for about two and a half years before his death. They had met when Garde-Wilson was working at a Melbourne-based law firm and was representing Caine on drink-driving charges.

Garde-Wilson was known as 'the Python with the hyphen' because she kept a snake in her office at the law firm. When it became apparent that an unnamed lawyer known as Lawyer X had been informing on members of the Melbourne underworld, there were rumours that it was Garde-Wilson. She vehemently denied this. In 2016, she filed an affidavit stating that she was aware of Lawyer X's identity, which was common knowledge in the legal fraternity, but she did not reveal it.

Lawyer X later emerged in a blaze of publicity as Nicola Gobbo, lawyer to bad men and niece of a former governor of Victoria. Gobbo was the youngest woman admitted to the bar in Australia. She grew up in Brighton, with all the privileges that bestows, but has become a blazing source of embarrassment to her illustrious family. She will go down in legal annals as the worst lawyer in our history.

In December 2018, Victorian Premier Daniel Andrews announced that the government was establishing a Royal Commission into the the Management of Police Informants to investigate police dealings with Gobbo. Garde-Wilson told the media that the use of Gobbo as a police informer had raised questions about several of her clients' prison sentences. She went on *A Current Affair* and pointed out that the lawyers and courts faced a daunting task, because they would need to unpack hundreds of cases involving some of Australia's most notorious criminals.

'These cases all need to be scrutinised one by one,' she said. 'Every single one of them needs to be wound back to find what did actually go on. Were they given a fair trial, and what are the consequences and results if they didn't?'

That's keeping the courts and lawyers busy. Some of those convictions have already been overturned, including one of the many convictions imposed on infamous drug kingpin Tony Mokbel, who was formerly a client of Garde-Wilson.

After Lewis Caine met his unfortunate end, Zarah partnered up with a young beau, Lansley Simon, who subsequently found himself facing charges for the murder of 38-year-old Paul Thornell at Cockatoo in Melbourne's east. It has been alleged that Simon had been bingeing on the drug ice before he fatally stabbed Thornell at his home.

While on remand at Port Phillip Prison awaiting trial, Simon complained about the conditions. Appearing by video link at a Supreme Court directions hearing into the matter, he told Justice Paul Coghlan that he objected to what he considered a delay in the legal system.

'That's a very long time to wait here in Port Phillip Prison,' Simon said. 'It's very unpleasant.'

Well, hullo! It ain't the Ritz!

When Simon's case came to court, the jury accepted his plea of self-defence and he was acquitted of murder. He and Garde-Wilson married in 2019 and have three children. They're good friends with Carl Williams' former wife Roberta and regularly release podcasts discussing criminal issues. In post-pandemic times, Simon has produced video-blogs under the moniker 'Lucky Lance' advancing various conspiracy theories about coronavirus. He claims that instead of masks and lockdowns, we need to quarantine the elderly and says the number of COVID-19 deaths is inflated because many of the elderly casualties 'would die of the hiccups'.

◆ ◆ ◆

Roberta Williams, or Bert as Carl used to call her, has become notorious for just being a gangster's wife. She had a tough childhood and swore to herself that she'd never be hungry or poor when she grew up. She came from behind, having been a state ward, then marrying an abusive man, getting into trouble with the police for drug trafficking, becoming friends with the Morans and eventually ditching her husband to marry Carl, who was known to the police as 'Fat Boy' and to Bert as Carlos or 'Fatty Boombah'.

They were an odd couple. She'd be photographed wearing Prada and Versace gear, which she bought on $25,000 shopping sprees to Europe, next to Carl with his round belly in trackie dacks or board shorts. But Carl provided her with the money and power she'd craved as a child. Her on-again, off-again romance with Williams, avidly reported in the media, made her famous in her own right. She has the cachet of being known by her first name only. Her every move is reported and her pithy epithets are repeatedly quoted. 'Famous, infamous, it's all the same,' she was once quoted as saying, and when she was jailed again for trafficking, she said, 'Who's going to hire me as a checkout chick?'

Williams was also adored by his mother, Barbara, who could see no wrong in her 'mummy's boy', even though he'd confessed to many of the gangland killings.

Barbara's life was haunted by tragedy. She lost her other son, Shane, to a heroin overdose in 1997. Then in 2006 and 2007, police successfully prosecuted Carl for a series of gangland killings. When he was sentenced in 2007, Barbara yelled at Judge Betty King, 'You are a puppet for corruption … a puppet for Purana', which was the taskforce investigating the killings. Barbara went on, 'You don't deserve your wig and gown!'

Barbara's estranged husband George was also jailed for several years after pleading guilty to trafficking commercial quantities of methamphetamine. With Carl and his father both in jail for the foreseeable future, Barbara became depressed. In November 2008, she took an overdose and was found dead. Adam Shand, who wrote about Melbourne's gangland wars, reflected, 'She has been depressed for some time. Her life has been on a downhill slope.' It's an understatement of monumental proportions.

The Carlos–Bert relationship was in an off period when Carl was sentenced, especially when he revealed that he'd started a new relationship with a young, pretty girl who'd written to him in prison. In a letter, Williams boasted to his furious wife, 'I can still pull 'em even when I'm in jail.' His attractiveness to women became another topic of discussion around some of Australia's dinner tables.

Williams was in protective custody with the two mates he'd chosen as 'trustworthy companions'. One of them had approval to speak on a phone hookup to Rocco Arico, a leading figure in Melbourne's gangland. It was widely known, mostly because it was canvassed by the media, that police intended to tap Carl Williams' knowledge of many of the hits that occurred during the gangland wars. He was also known to be helping police with their inquiries into a Victorian detective's alleged involvement in a double murder to silence an informer.

Bert was also hoping he'd sing like a canary, because police had promised Carl that they'd send his nine-year-old daughter Dhakota to a private school and pay off a million-dollar debt George Williams owed the tax office, among other perks. This would lift a cloud over her father-in-law's home, where she and Dhakota were living. A perfect life really: a troublesome husband in jail indefinitely, providing a high life funded by

Vicpol while he shafted his associates. Had he lived, Carl may also have been instrumental in solving a lot of serious crimes.

But a singing Carl held too much danger for those with money, power and influence. It is believed that Rocco Arico used his association with one of Carl's cellmates to persuade him to encourage Matthew Johnson, Carl's other cellmate, to bash Carl to death. Unfortunately, police did not pick up the other inmate's connection with Arico or the approved phone link to him. Carl had his back turned and was reading the paper when Johnson sneaked up behind him with a sharpened metal rod he'd taken from an exercise bike, while the other cellmate looked on and the nearby guard wandered off somewhere for a few minutes.

One may well ask, where *were* the guards? This was happening in protective custody at one of the toughest, most secure prisons in Victoria.

For murdering Carl Williams, Matthew Johnson got thirty-two years on top of his earlier sentence. 'I acted alone,' he said in his police interview. But police later discovered that substantial amounts of money had been paid into the bank accounts of some people associated with Carl's two cellmates.

On hearing the news of Carl's death, Bert shed an appropriate amount of tears, then the Carlos–Bert relationship was on again. Bert had her hair done and set to arranging for a gold-plated copy of Elvis Presley's coffin to come from the USA. With Carl's body inside, it was so heavy that it had to be wheeled in and eight strong men struggled to carry it out. She also wrote a eulogy at the funeral describing him as 'a family man', and put Dhakota, the only child of her union with Carl, on display to read a tribute to her murdering and murdered father.

Talking of his efforts to tease Bert, Dhakota said, 'You thought you were funny, but you weren't.' Out of the mouths of babes …

The card on the coffin read: 'A loving dad, husband, son, brother and friend whose smile will never be replaced. 13.10.1970 to 19.4.2010. A special smile, a special face, a special man we can't replace. Just think of Carl as resting from the sorrow and the tears in a place of warmth and comfort where there are no days and years.'

Pity about all the other 'family men' Williams murdered. Bert seems to have forgotten about them.

◆ ◆ ◆

Why do smart, attractive women gravitate towards crooks and gangsters? Alex Bartsch, a former Homicide cop and commentator on Melbourne's gangland wars, divides gangster groupies into types. 'There are the Florence Nightingales who befriend and defend the people society despises, much the way they might save a lost dog. These women think they can rescue, "cure" or change bad men,' he said. Zarah Garde-Wilson seems to fit that mould. Lewis Caine had been convicted of murder before they met, and even after his death, she remained friendly with gangland members. Defending her legal representation of crime figures, she has said, 'Someone has to do it.'

Garde-Wilson refused to testify at the trial of Caine's killers on the grounds that giving evidence would put her life at risk. She was convicted of contempt of court, and further charged with illegal possession of Caine's unregistered gun. She was also charged with four counts of giving false evidence to the Australian Crime Commission.

She paid a high price for her silence, losing her licence to practise law in Victoria. In the publicity surrounding the case, she was also reported to have been close to another client, convicted cocaine trafficker Tony Mokbel, who fled Australia during his trial and was later extradited from Greece to face a new charge of killing rival drug lord Lewis Moran. Garde-Wilson denied the claim that she was close to Mokbel, and it has never been substantiated.

Eventually, she was able to rehabilitate her situation. The firearms and perjury charges against her were dropped, and the Legal Services Board restored her certificate to practise. She has since been appointed to the bar and established a successful legal practice specialising in criminal law, of which she has broad experience.

Interviewed after Victoria's royal commission into the Lawyer X scandal, Garde-Wilson let go with both barrels on *A Current Affair*. She spoke of how her client, Carl Williams, had been railroaded by the criminal justice system.

Her criticisms, she said, were not about whether Williams was guilty or innocent of the crimes he was convicted of, but about whether the judicial system had acted fairly to put him away.

'All of Carl's trials were so corrupt to the core, and that's all come out with the royal commission,' she said. She alleged her notorious client 'was not afforded proper representation or a fair trial' in any of his proceedings after 2004.

She described Nicola Gobbo's role in putting Williams away as 'the biggest affront to justice you can imagine'.

She lambasted Victoria's judicial process as 'disgracefully corrupted for over a decade' and labelled police actions 'an affront to justice'. She did, however, qualify her criticisms by saying, 'This isn't Victoria Police as a whole, this is a group of police officers who chose to ignore the law, ignore justice, and take a line of policing which is illegal and corrupt.'

As someone who has spent the last quarter-century trying to promote truth and justice in the legal system, I agree with Ms Garde-Wilson to a degree. The processes used to convict Carl Williams were an abuse of the system. At the same time, he deserved to be convicted. He was a nasty and vengeful killer who didn't show his victims much mercy. He lived by the sword, and deserved what he got.

◆ ◆ ◆

There was a twist to the Williams story. After the death of George Williams, Roberta and her teenage daughter Dhakota were living in the family's Essendon house, which George had left to Dhakota in his will. But they faced increasing pressure from the tax office, which claimed George had died owing them a large sum of money. The amount involved was $740,000 at George's death, but it had since risen to just under $1 million. When Victoria Police were dealing with Carl as an informer, they'd promised him they'd pay this bill, but he was killed before they got their money's worth. No-one from Vicpol came forward to honour the deal, so the bill remained unpaid and the tax office served them with an eviction notice.

Roberta appealed, citing Carl's alleged agreement with the police, but the tax office said it had no involvement in Carl's deal. The court said the appeal had no merit, was bound to fail and ought to be dismissed in its entirety. The house was seized and sold in December 2018.

On the eleventh anniversary of Carl's death, Roberta posted footage on Instagram of her wedding to Carl, where they were looking very young indeed. She wrote:

> *You were my strength, my best friend, my light in the dark and my umbrella in the rain. You never let me fall, you always caught me. My love, my life, my best friend, my baby daddy, my husband. I miss you immensely! Shine bright like a diamond.*

Roberta would have made a good copywriter for Hallmark cards.

The gangland wars seem to have attracted an exotic mix of wives and girlfriends. Once these women only made headlines in Melbourne, usually when they were weeping over the latest casualty, but with the popularity of TV series based on the gangland killings and the intricate relationships involved, people all around Australia now feel on first-name terms with many of the widows and wives. One story of a woman's involvement in assisting a criminal made headlines around the world – the escape while on bail of the notorious Tony Mokbel.

Now-retired judge Bill Gillard presided over Mokbel's trial, and it was on his watch that Mokbel absconded in March 2006, just as the jury was about to begin deliberating on his guilt or innocence. Judge Gillard allowed Mokbel's bail to continue until the end of the trial, which he ruefully admits now was a costly mistake.

In Mokbel's absence, he was convicted of importing cocaine, and Gillard sentenced him to twelve years in jail, with a minimum of nine. But first they had to catch him.

Ironically, for the first few months after his escape, Mokbel hung out in a farmhouse about two hours' drive from Melbourne in the hills around Bonnie Doon, the area made famous by the Jenny Tanner case. Tony may have been smiling at all the fuss he'd caused, but his sister-in-law, Renate, wasn't happy at all. She was married to Tony's brother Milad, who was in jail awaiting his own trial on drug-related issues, and she'd offered $1 million surety to guarantee Tony's bail. Now Justice Gillard wanted her to pay up, and to pay the huge Crown legal bill.

Justice Gillard was not impressed with Renate. He described her as 'a liar and a witness with no credibility' and made scathing remarks about the Mokbel family. Renate appealed the severity of his orders, but she didn't come to court in one of the designer outfits that had drawn the attention of the tabloid media during Tony's trial. In fact, she didn't show up at all, leaving her appeal to her lawyers on the grounds of financial hardship. Renate earned $700 a week in the hairdressing shop she ran with Mokbel's girlfriend Danielle McGuire, but her lawyers told the court her monthly expenses totalled nearly $6000. Justice Gillard was not impressed. In her absence, he dismissed her application. He said she'd not been honest about the full extent of her assets or how her family came by them.

During the hearings that led up to that day, police had discovered drug paraphernalia and large sums of cash at her home. She explained the cash by saying that her husband was a 'good gambler'. Justice Gillard said this was 'laughable, defied belief and a deliberate lie'. Three months before the hearing, a separate police raid on her uncle's home unearthed nearly $350,000 in cash buried in the backyard, along with a hundred pieces of expensive jewellery, estimated to be worth $200,000. More of Milad's 'good gambling' proceeds, no doubt.

Justice Gillard said that Tony Mokbel was 'a strong, arrogant and determined man and a very dishonest criminal', and that Renate's 'loyalty to him and his family outweighed any obligation she felt to the court'. Another woman standing by her man, or men, in this case.

Renate had put up her house as a bail collateral for Tony, but during an appeal she lodged into the severity of her two-year prison sentence, it turned out that police had seized it as property bought with immoral earnings, so she didn't own it any more. The police were getting crankier by the minute at being fooled by Mokbel, and they were certain that Renate had known he was going to disappear and perhaps even knew where he was. She was charged with perjury and perverting the course of justice for lying about her assets. She was already in prison, but she was taken back to face more music in court. The charges had the potential to add another three years to her sentence. Police seemed to be venting their frustration about Tony on Renate.

Renate's four-year-old son periodically shared a cell with his mother, because he faced 'extensive difficulties' being without her, while her two older children stayed with her mother. One wonders at the selflessness of the mothers of these women, having little children thrust upon them in the autumn of their lives – and what the children think of it all. Media reports about Renate in jail called her 'a broken woman'. I heard on the grapevine I should try to get in and talk to her. I was told she was seething with the injustice of her treatment and ready to download, but I passed on that tip.

The Mokbel story continues. For some unaccountable reason, this plain little bloke with an ugly past seems to be a chick magnet. His attractive blonde girlfriend, Danielle McGuire, allegedly put money into London bank accounts for him, then quietly left Australia with her nine-year-old daughter, giving the police the slip and joining Mokbel in his Greek hideaway. She has stood by him ever since, through extradition and other serious charges while Tony waited his turn in the supposedly safe-custody cells at Barwon, where Carl Williams was bashed to death. Mokbel is now serving the sentence handed down by Justice Gillard at Barwon prison, although that conviction may be in doubt owing to information that has surfaced about Nicola Gobbo's role in his downfall.

I've seen Mokbel sometimes when I'm visiting another prisoner at Barwon, his bald head shining in the sun as he does laps of the outside area, or hosting family-style visits around a large table inside. You wouldn't look twice at him in the street. He got nine years. The various women in his life are hoping he'll make it.

So ... Nicola Gobbo. A big book has been written about Ms Gobbo and her part in the conviction of Tony Mokbel and his friends, among many others. The title is *Lawyer X*, because for many months the journalist who uncovered her dealings with the police and her clients was not permitted to name her.

Police went to extraordinary lengths to protect her identity, right up to the High Court. Some who had been in very senior positions during her time as Informer 3838 later gave sworn evidence to the royal commission that they weren't aware that Gobbo was being run as an informant. (This was later shown to be incorrect.)

By Gobbo's own estimation, the information she gleaned from her clients accounted for nearly 400 arrests. The royal commission placed the figure much higher, estimating that more than a thousand people could have their convictions reviewed.

This means that any or all of those prisoners, some doing very long sentences, could have the right to appeal their convictions, citing unfair representation and perverting the course of justice, which carries a sentence of up to twenty-five years. Oops! Even if they are guilty as convicted, they can appeal on the grounds that Gobbo's informing led to a miscarriage of justice.

The first appeal to succeed as a result of Gobbo's misconduct was that of Faruk Orman, whose conviction was overturned in July 2019. Orman was twenty-five years old when he was found guilty of murdering gangster Victor Peirce in 2002. Alleged to be the getaway driver in the murder, he spent twelve years in jail, a large chunk of it involving mistreatment by prison officers and lengthy periods of solitary confinement.

Orman told the ABC's *7.30*, 'Even after I got convicted, I used to try to convince myself that eventually the truth will come out ... but it crushes you.'

Mr Orman claims that while Ms Gobbo was working as his lawyer, she fed information back to police about his defence strategy. Nice person to have on your side!

Many more convictions have been challenged, including those of Tony Mokbel himself.

After several hearings, a royal commission, changes of police commissioners, being denied by the police and fingered by the crooks, Gobbo and her two small children are now out of sight. No-one is saying where they are, other than that it's probably somewhere with a warm climate.

At the time of writing this, Gobbo's life is probably not in danger, because crooks who've been done over by her would need to call her as a witness if there was a trial. But once she's satisfied those requirements, she'll need to stay very well hidden.

◆ ◆ ◆

Some prison WAGs seem to revel in their vicarious notoriety, seeing it as a chance to star in their own soap operas as the cameras roll outside courts and gangland funerals. Gangland matriarch Judy Moran often attended courts in carefully chosen (but not very flattering!) outfits and black lace stockings to hear charges against those who had admitted murdering both her sons and her former husband.

Despite the violent deaths of most of the men in her family, Moran always had a smart quote for reporters, her blonde curls carefully coiffed and most of her face hidden behind celebrity sunnies.

'Like their men, some mobster women are full-blown narcissists with delusions of grandeur,' says Alex Bartsch. 'They have an over-inflated sense of entitlement, lack of empathy and disregard for consequences.'

In keeping with her celebrity status, Moran signed a contract with publicist Harry M. Miller and announced she'd be writing a book about her life, including a section 'clearing the name' of her recently murdered estranged partner, Lewis Moran. Police were aghast, claiming she shouldn't be allowed to profit from her family's nefarious activities.

She got a Harry M. Miller-sized advance and wrote the book, which was released in February 2005 with an appropriate PR splash. Unfortunately for the publishers, it contained some allegedly false stories about a dead cop whose son objected strongly, so all 20,000 hard-cover copies were withdrawn and pulped. An amended re-release sold about 5000 copies.

Moran was finally charged with the murder of Des Moran, Lewis's brother, who was shot dead in 2009 while drinking coffee outside a cafe in an inner-suburban shopping strip near her home. There must have been a tip-off, as police already had her under surveillance. They were watching as she hid the killers' getaway car in her garage and then abandoned it in a nearby street. She was arrested as she walked home.

The police discovered a rifle in the abandoned car and found the white gloves Judy Moran was allegedly wearing discarded in bushes nearby. A subsequent search warrant on her home uncovered a hidden safe containing three handguns, two stolen Victorian licence plates, a wig and clothing that police claimed matched witness descriptions of clothing worn by the gunmen. Moran might have thought she was glamorous and smart, but most crooks are stupid. That's why they get caught.

On 9 March 2011, a jury found Judy Moran guilty of murdering Desmond Moran. She got twenty-six years with a twenty-one-year minimum, so she will almost certainly die in jail. I've seen her around on my visits to other inmates in the women's prison. She cuts a pathetic figure; an old, embittered woman in a wheelchair. She doesn't make waves anymore, nor does she get any.

◆ ◆ ◆

Many prisoners' women have their men where they want them. The women call the shots. With their partners in prison, they don't have to worry about where they are and what they're up to, because they know. They don't have to shop, feed or clean up after these men, let alone cop beltings from them, and rough sex is a distant memory. The women can just visit once a week. They don't have to tolerate drunkenness or drug dealing in their homes. To men serving time, the women's loyalty is sustaining, but it doesn't always last when they get out.

Retired standover man Mark 'Chopper' Read, who had dozens of female admirers while he was in prison, was quoted in a *Sunday Age* article as saying, 'Jail romances sour quickly on the outside'. He said that women who fall in love and marry men in jail find they don't want to associate with their husbands when they get out. Read added, 'Like the great man said – I don't want to belong to any club that will have me as a member.'

But it seems the more notorious the criminal, the more women line up to see him. A surprising number of attractive women are available to felons, though they aren't in the public spotlight. Some couples meet through prison visits, exchange letters or speak over the phone. Typically, it's the woman reaching out to the man. But why? What's the attraction? Bank robbers, murderers, rapists and serial killers don't seem like the kind of people women would want to have a relationship with. But many are attracted to the danger, and all are fascinated by the bad men of their desires.

Some women move miles away from family and friends to be with men in prison. This has become more onerous as prisons in many country towns have closed and big suburban jails such as Melbourne's

Pentridge and Boggo Road in Brisbane have been replaced by new prisons in remote locations. For a woman who doesn't drive, it can take two or three hours each way to visit a man in jail.

Women who love men behind bars find it rules their lives. Their daily routine tends to revolve around jail visitation hours, making parenting, work and day-to-day living far more difficult than they would normally be. These women play the victim time and time again, and their relationships with prisoners can have disastrous effects on their children and their wider families.

How does something like this happen? Most women who fall in love with bad men have one thing in common: they are insecure. They want someone to love them, and they want to feel wanted. They're usually lonely; they don't have many friends, and they rarely have strong ties with family. Women who love bad men are looking for danger, excitement and unconditional love. Criminals commonly have all these traits, which is why women fall for them.

◆ ◆ ◆

Sometimes a woman who is in love with a criminal becomes involved in helping them to break out of jail or commits crimes even as serious as attempted murder. Some live the high life at other people's expense or traffic in other women as slaves for men's pleasure.

Tania Herman gained Australia-wide notoriety as the 'body in the boot' girl. She fell in love with a sinister conman by the name of Joe Korp and was so much under his spell that she was persuaded to lie in wait for his wife Maria in the garage of their family home, ambush her when she left for work, stuff her body in the car boot and abandon it in the middle of Melbourne. Still alive but mortally injured, Maria suffered alone in the boot of the hot car until it was spotted four days later. It was several days before Maria died in hospital, with Joe playing the grieving husband by her side.

Why did Tania do this dreadful thing? I spoke to her in prison when I was writing my book *Jail Birds*, and she told the story as if it was the most natural thing to have done at the time. By the time I spoke to her, however, she'd overcome her feelings for this creep, who had allegedly killed himself (though Tania thinks he had help) rather than face the consequences of their murderous plot, leaving Tania to bear the full responsibility. Awful as it seems, she wanted the truth told so she could do her time and get out with some semblance of a life left.

Another woman who was induced to commit a crime was Lucy Dudko, who became known as 'the helicopter bandit'. A young woman of Russian extraction, Lucy fell for a lovable knockabout recidivist crook called John Killick. Killick was married with a young son, and when Lucy met him he was out of jail. She moved in with him and his family, but then John was nabbed (yet again) for robbing a bank and sent to Sydney's Silverwater prison. His ever-pragmatic wife, Gloria, was getting on without him as she did when he went to jail, but Lucy couldn't bear to lose him. Using amazing panache and coolness, she hijacked a helicopter while ostensibly on a joyride and forced the pilot to descend into the prison exercise yard. John had been alerted to be on standby, and she scooped him out from among his gob-smacked fellow prisoners. The guards were scared to fire in case they hit the pilot and brought the chopper crashing down on top of everyone. John and Lucy were on the run. And did they have fun! They were eventually caught and John went back to jail. So did she. She became religious and went into near-seclusion, eschewing her life of crime. One way to deal with the fallout, I suppose.

Jody Harris, Australia's own 'catch me if you can' girl, was a specialist in identity theft; one of her tricks was to steal money and identifying information from the purses of plane passengers sitting beside her when they went to the toilet. The purse would be returned to the neighbour's bag a lot lighter. By the time her victims discovered that their credit cards and driver's licences had disappeared, they'd been maxed out and Jody had moved on.

Jody's mother, Debbie Kilroy, also did jail time because of her relationship with a man she loved. Debbie has become a friend since

I met her years ago on a speakers' panel. She was brought up in Brisbane, and her childhood was punctuated by abuse and stints in juvenile prison. At the age of twenty-five, she married a rugby league star who was nicknamed 'Smokin' Joe Kilroy' because of his great speed on the football field. Joe was a drug user and small-time dealer, and he enlisted Debbie to his cause, but her dealing career was cut short when she tried to sell cannabis to some undercover police. In 1989, she was sentenced to six years in jail.

Her prison experience was searing. At one point, she was wounded in Boggo Road jail when she was seated beside a friend who was stabbed to death by sharpened forks. While she was behind bars, she got a degree in social work, and on her release she set up a prisoner advocacy program, Sisters Inside. This is now a nationwide organisation, advocating for women prisoners and their children, and helping women to a safer, better life when they're behind bars and when they get out.

Debbie went on to study law and became one of the few practising lawyers who'd ever been convicted for drug offences. This feat stunned many in the legal community, because lawyers are generally prohibited from practising if they have a prior conviction.

'How did you pull that off?' I asked her, being married to a lawyer myself at the time.

She replied, 'I went straight to the top. Attorney General, other ministers. Asked them if rehab was a fairytale they spun for the media, or did they want a real live example?'

Meanwhile, Jody had gone off the rails. It happens in the best families. She stole credit cards and drivers' licences from many sources and withdrew large sums of money from her victims' bank accounts. She used stolen credit cards to spend lavishly, splashing out on plane tickets, high-end rent, designer goods, expensive handbags, luxury car hires and hotels.

Jody travelled from Queensland to Melbourne, living the high life on other women's money. During her one-woman crime spree across three states, she posed as a doctor, psychologist, businesswoman, undercover policewoman, flight attendant and even the niece of slain underworld figure Mario Condello.

Nova Gordon, the owner of a Melbourne clothing boutique, said Harris had posed as a wealthy seafood wholesaler and bought a $600 dress from her, then invited her for a coffee. Afterwards, Nova realised that her driver's licence had been stolen. She soon discovered that it had been used to withdraw $80,000 from her account.

In a press release delivered to the media after Jody's arrest, Detective Inspector Grant Taylor of Rose Bay police said, 'We are interviewing her in relation to her assuming the identity of numerous women throughout New South Wales and in respect to her having items in her possession that were unlawfully obtained.'

On a flight between Melbourne and Brisbane, she sat next to a flight attendant and lifted her driver's licence, which allowed her to take $22,000 from the woman's bank account. When the teller asked Jody her birthday, she coolly said, 'It's there, on my driver's licence.' She got the money.

She was an opportunist, always at the ready. When a woman fell on the footpath in Sydney and injured her head, Jody stepped up. 'I'm a doctor,' she said and took the injured woman to hospital, nicking her driver's licence on the way.

She was in a relationship with a serving Victorian police officer, Senior Constable Andrew Twining, who was apparently unaware of his glamorous girlfriend's source of income. Jody had told him she worked as a hostess at Virgin Blue, and she used this to explain her frequent trips away, when she defrauded women from Brisbane to Melbourne.

The Sydney police began closing in on Jody after she visited a letting agent in Cremorne, apparently to rent a furnished executive apartment in Neutral Bay.

The property manager said later that Jody was 'extremely well groomed ... At first no-one picked her, but one of the ladies who works here suddenly twigged.' Apparently, Jody became edgy when a staff member asked to photocopy her identification documents. Jody said she had to go outside to get money for the bond from her husband, who was waiting in a car, but she didn't return. Detecting danger with the antennae of a con artist, Jody had fled. Police found her hire car parked in a street out the back of the office the next morning.

The letting agent said Jody rang her the next day, posing as a senior police officer. 'She said she was Detective Sergeant such-and-such ... I told her everything, how I picked up on her. I was even joking about all the diamonds on her fingers. I was on the phone to her for ten minutes, then she suddenly hung up on me. I felt like such a fool.' Police later told this woman her information had been crucial in helping them arrest Harris.

By this stage, police in three states were looking for a woman who was befriending other women, stealing their identities and withdrawing large sums from their bank accounts. Eventually, they realised that they were all chasing the same person.

Senior Constable Twining was on an international cruise with his parents when his Victorian colleagues told him what Jody was up to. By that stage, she'd realised her cover was blown and had gone on the run, teasing police by sending them text messages and photographs of herself as she went. They were pursuing her, but she kept slipping through their fingers.

Harris was so sure of her ability to avoid detection that she phoned the police in Victoria and offered to turn herself in, but then backed out at the last minute.

When Senior Constable Twining discovered what she'd done, he offered to help the Sydney police catch her when he came back to Australia.

On his return, he phoned Jody and arranged to meet her in Ultimo in his car. When she got into his car, the police struck.

They raided her apartment, where they found wigs and other items of disguise, along with more than a hundred drivers' licences, passports, Medicare cards, bank cards, mobile phone SIM cards and police identification documents. The arresting officers refused to say which police service the documents belonged to. Police also seized a Virgin Blue flight attendant's uniform and name tag.

Jody Harris was charged with thirty-four counts of obtaining money by deception and one count of larceny. Initially, the vast number of identification documents made it hard for the police to confirm her identity, because they couldn't work out who she was.

After her arrest, it was revealed that she'd previously produced a stolen police badge and convinced officers from Victoria's CIB that she was an undercover drug operative from Queensland. Police sources claimed that on at least one occasion she was welcomed into the inner sanctum, where she was provided with confidential investigation details, issued with a gun and accompanied officers on a raid.

Christine Nixon, Victoria's chief commissioner, told the fascinated media that those claims were under investigation. 'We don't have any evidence that she may have been supplied with a firearm or that she became an undercover agent for Victoria Police,' she said. Ms Nixon confirmed that they would extradite Harris once she'd faced court in New South Wales.

The grapevine said that Harris had agreed to demonstrate her skills to help authorities catch future perpetrators. I heard she'd participated in a training video detailing her crimes and explaining how she avoided detection. I thought, I'd like to see that!

I contacted one of the officers involved in her arrest and we met at a coffee shop behind the St Kilda Road police headquarters. Unfortunately, the response to my request to watch the video was a definite 'No'. It would have made interesting viewing.

Jody eventually pleaded guilty to assuming the identities of at least fifteen women. During her lavish career, she'd stolen $70,000 in Queensland, about $175,000 from thirty-three victims in New South Wales and more again in Victoria. She was eventually sentenced to five years in jail, with a non-parole period of three-and-a-half. If she served her full sentence, that would be about $50,000 a year from known crimes. It seemed to be hard work for that kind of money.

Further reading

The full stories of some of the women mentioned in this chapter can be found in my book *Jail Birds*, which is available online and from major distributors.

Chapter Three

'HE WAS SO BEAUTIFUL'

A woman by the name of Josie wrote to me through my website saying she wanted to tell me her story, because she thought she might write a book about her experiences. She wasn't ready to do it at the time, but she agreed to work with me on a short piece that would tell her side of the story. It was three years since her beloved boyfriend, John Xydias, had been sent to prison for twenty-eight years. When she talked about him, she still got teary, and she was indignant about the charges against him. At the same time, she was angry with him for being so stupid, for being unfaithful and for leaving her alone. But she still missed him, loved him and was living most of her days in the past, because the future was too bleak to contemplate.

Police arrested John Xydias in Melbourne in 2007 after they were shown a video of some women and girls, including one very attractive girl, preening themselves, fixing their hair, putting on lipstick and adjusting their clothing, all behaving unselfconsciously in front of the camera, because they didn't know it was there. The camera had been fitted into a hole in the wall, hidden in the female changing room at a restaurant where John Xydias was working as a chef. The footage was one way he got his jollies from watching women without their knowledge.

Josie's parents and grandparents had come to Australia from Europe as part of the wave of families seeking a new future after World War II. They had a long and productive history in Australia, building businesses and having families of their own.

Josie's mum sounded quite indignant when I asked how her 45-year-old daughter had become caught up in such a strange relationship. She said, 'I told her, get rid of this man! I hated his guts. I love my two girls so dearly, I look after them for everything. I don't want to tell her what to do. But why does she go with this man?'

Josie couldn't give her mother any answers and felt guilty that things had turned out this way. 'I've shamed myself and I've shamed my family,' she told me. For this reason, she didn't want me to use her family name.

Josie's mother lived nearby, but all Josie had to keep her company at home were a cat, a bookshelf full of dolls in national costume, and dozens of stuffed toys.

When I first visited, there were so many fluffy toys that I thought maybe she had a child. A big stuffed Mickey Mouse was occupying the seat next to Josie's, and opposite it was a child-sized space, but I soon established that there were no other signs of children.

Josie was a big woman, well built, not fat, with long, bleached hair and several intricate tattoos. After the mandatory Italian kiss-and-coffee routine, she disappeared into the kitchen to make a proper Italian coffee, leaving me to have a good look around.

The lounge was small and sparsely furnished. I moved the (real) Somali Abyssinian cat out of the way and parked myself on a black vinyl couch. There were two matching armchairs opposite, a TV and a huge boom box on a dining table against the far wall.

Josie returned with the aromatic coffee and we settled in for a chat. She told me yellow was her favourite colour, pointing out her yellow 'hope' symbol and the weeping Madonna of Guadalupe that decorated the walls. As well as being the patron saint of Mexico and South America, the Madonna of Guadalupe is the emblem of Sicily, where Josie's family originated. On her wall, the Madonna's tears flowed liberally into her exposed red heart. 'She's crying for me and John,' Josie said.

Josie was anxious to set the record straight about her involvement in John's arrest. She assured me that her role was unintentional. All she wanted was for him to give up smoking dope to excess.

In the event, he received a jail term that will separate him from her for pretty much the rest of her life. Josie was forty-one when John was sentenced and will be sixty-one when he's released, but she'd promised to stay true to him. 'I sometimes wish there were two Josies, like twins,' she told me tearfully. 'One to visit John and love and support him and the other one, still a young woman, to begin a new life before I get too old.' She sounded sad, and her mood didn't really improve during my visit. Women in love with men in prison serve their own sentence on the outside.

This is her story as she told it.

Josie was thirty-three when she met John in 1998. She described herself as 'a good Italian girl, no record or anything like that'. She was slim and looked interesting. She had been nicely brought up; her marriage had recently been annulled and she had no children. She was blonde, more convincingly then than now, from the photos she showed me.

Six weeks after her annulment had come through, she was looking for some company and tried a telephone dating service, which was where she encountered John. They spoke to each other on the phone during a two-week phone foreplay before they arranged to meet.

They met outside the Harold Holt pool in Malvern, a leafy middle-class Liberal stronghold in Melbourne's eastern suburbs. It was near John's Glen Iris home, where he was still living with his parents in his mid-thirties, and it was also close to where Josie lived.

'It was an instant attraction,' Josie said. 'We left the baths and drove to St Kilda Beach carpark and then I went and sat with him in his beautiful sports car and talked for ages. Eventually, John gave me a kiss on the cheek, hugged me and said, "I'm so glad I met you, Josie." He was such a perfect gentleman. He was so beautiful. Blonde hair, great body.' She'd fallen for him straight away.

Unfortunately for Josie, she wasn't the first susceptible woman John Xydias had met through the dating service, and she wouldn't be the only one during their nine-year on-again, off-again relationship.

Josie was keen for me to look through several albums full of photos of her lover. I had to admit that when they met he didn't look too bad. He was well built, with a full head of bleached blonde hair brushed back like a mane. I could tell he was proud of his strong physique from the skimpy jocks he wore and the body-builder poses he adopted in many of the photos. He was naked in quite a few of them. In one, he had a pair of Ray-Bans perched on the only spot other than his nose where there was a protrusion.

The later photos were less flattering. By the time of his trial, he looked much worse for wear. Time and gravity, hair loss and indulgence in drugs had taken their toll.

John was the only child of a Greek couple who had come to Australia after the war. They had a pleasant house in Glen Iris and a holiday house in Dromana on the Mornington Peninsula, about fifty minutes' drive from the city, a favourite destination for Melburnians on holiday. Many holiday-makers visit the coastal township every year, pitch a tent or park a caravan in the same reserved camping site, and spend school holidays next to the same people while all their kids grow up together. The Xydias family had done well enough to buy a house in the town, and John used it frequently. But when he visited, his mind wasn't on a holiday in the sunshine. His pursuits were darker, lit by spotlights trained on his choice of entertainment – unconscious women.

Josie was unaware of his obsession. She told me that she willingly (never as a victim as far as she knew) took part in several videos that showed her in lovely lingerie, photos of which were scattered throughout the albums. To please John, she also allowed their lovemaking to be filmed. It never occurred to her that she wasn't the only one. 'He bought me a ring,' she said. 'I wanted to marry him.'

But John Xydias turned out to be a subscriber to the maxim, 'Why buy a book, when you can join a library?'

'They called John the "rag-doll rapist",' Josie told me, 'but I want the public to see John as I saw him — a beautiful person with a heart. I'll give you an example,' she said earnestly. 'He found out I like mangoes. One day, he just sneaked up behind me with — *a case of mangoes*! How lovely is that?' She clapped her hands like a little kid. The memory cheered her up for a while.

She told me John had gone to a good school — Wesley College — and then trained as a chef at William Angliss College, one of Australia's leading catering training schools. He quickly obtained work in the industry, and for several years he followed his first employer around from one Greek restaurant to another, working three days a week. He had lots of spare time.

The only sour note in Josie's relationship with John was his addiction to marijuana. In the beginning, Josie went along with her lover's heavy consumption from the never-ending supply he hid in his bedroom, but as time wore on, she felt he was taking it to excess. She tried many times to persuade him to stop, or at least cut down, but to no avail.

One day when she was visiting John's family for a meal, she and Mrs Xydias were having a girls-together in the kitchen. Josie told John's mother he was addicted to dope and suggested that Mrs Xydias should take him in hand and make him stop. Josie said she was concerned for John's future welfare if he kept smoking such large quantities. 'He might get in trouble with the police, even,' Josie said.

John's mother was furious. She rounded on Josie and told her John was a good boy. No trouble, especially with the police. She said Josie was no longer welcome in their home, and she made a few remarks about her bleached hair and her tatts as well — remarks Josie hadn't forgiven. After that, Josie only visited the Xydias's Glen Iris home when John's parents were away. But she still visited Dromana often, and John spent a lot of time at her place.

Although John often proclaimed his love for Josie, he had a strange obsession with Naomi Robson, an attractive TV presenter who was then hosting Channel 7's *Today Tonight* program in the eastern states. While he never actually stalked her, he collected photos of her, filmed her programs, and got Josie to write her a fan letter, which elicited a signed photo 'To John from Naomi'. Though Josie wasn't aware of this, John allegedly pasted photocopied cut-outs of Naomi's face onto pornographic photos of naked or near-naked women taken from the files he'd assembled. He also made masks from a blown-up photo of her face and persuaded Josie to wear one during sex. He was devastated when Naomi stopped presenting *Today Tonight* at the end of 2006.

'It all started with Naomi Robson,' Josie told me. 'John saw a TV promotion that said Naomi was going to be on TV on *Dancing with the Stars* in March 2007.' He was excited to see her dance in the first two programs and filmed the show.

John had to work the night of the third show, Josie said. 'So, because his DVD recorder was playing up, he asked me to record the show. I said I would. I was always recording stuff for him – we've got every gangster movie ever – but I was getting low on my empty discs, so I said, "Well, you'd better bring me a new one, or I might run out when you want something else recorded." It was just a joke, really. I would have done *anything* for him back then.'

Josie recorded the program, and two nights later John came around. He collected the disc and handed over a shiny new replacement. They watched the show together, then John left with the recording to add to his Naomi collection.

The following day, Josie bought a new hard drive tower for her computer. She needed something with more grunt to cope with storing all the movies and other files.

The next evening, she was alone because John was working – 'or I *think* he was working, she says. 'I'm never sure now if I was told truth or lies.' So she decided to try it out by re-recording a borrowed copy of *Scarface*. 'One of my all-time favourite movies,' she said. 'I *love* Al Pacino!' (I'd gathered that from the life-size poster hanging on the wall behind the international dolls.)

'I got the disc John had brought me, pressed the "burn" button on the tower and the screen kept going grey. It wouldn't record. So I tried it on the old tower and looked at the screen. "What's this?" I asked myself. "Not *Scarface*!" Although the speaker was on, there was no sound. It was just silent. There were girls dancing around, putting on their makeup. One even did a star jump – she was happy about something. They went in and out of range, making me think the camera was fixed. I just stared at it for so long. *Omigod*! I thought. *Omigod*!

'I knew straight away what it was. I recognised the change rooms from the restaurant where John was working. It was the female staff dressing room. A girl put on a restaurant T-shirt and I absolutely knew. "Omigod! How did John get this?" I asked myself.'

Josie watched the footage several times. She was trying to imagine how John could have got this material but not be responsible for filming it, but, in her heart of hearts, she knew he had. It had John Xydias stamped all over it.

'I spent hours and hours smoking and thinking what to do. From 1 am to 8 am, I just thought and thought. I rang my mum. She said, "Burn it! Break it! Don't get involved." But I started to think this might be a good way to get John off marijuana. His parents wouldn't help me, or actually help *him*, so I thought I'd have to do it myself. I decided to ring the police.

'Honest to God, I thought they might go round and search his bedroom and find all the dope and he might get a little warning and some rehab. That's all I thought.'

She rang her local police station at 8.30 am and asked them to send plainclothes police around. 'I don't want any police cars or uniforms. I'm a good girl and I have a good name.'

Soon afterwards, two detectives arrived. They viewed some of the disc and took custody of it. One told Josie on no account to say anything to John about his visit or her phone call to the police. As they left, they warned her again. 'Say nothing to John about calling us.'

Josie was gutted. Exhausted and tearful, she pulled her curtains shut against the world and fell into bed.

'It was so difficult not saying anything to John,' she went on. 'I was scared about what I'd done on impulse, you know. Whenever he came round during those following few days, I could hardly keep a straight face.

'Later in the week, I was down at his place in Dromana and I saw a photo on the buffet of one of the entertainers from John's restaurant – from the video! I had to bite my lip to stop me shouting at him.'

Several days later, Detective Senior Constable Matthew Graiff called Josie.

'He said they needed to come and see me straight away. I was terrified.'

Detective Graiff came to her condo with a colleague, Detective Allen, and they questioned her for four hours.

'All the questions were about videos and filmed stuff,' she told me. 'There were lots of questions about a video camera, but not about the DVD I'd given them. Detective Allen kept shaking his head. He seemed to think I knew all about it. He said that they'd seen DVDs and that they'd had John in there all the day before.'

She told them, 'If there was a girl getting raped when I was there, I have morals. I would have stopped it immediately. I would have got her out of the house, or I would have made her run real fast.'

The police told Josie they'd executed search warrants on the Glen Iris home and the house in Dromana. They'd found lots and lots of pornographic videos in the bedroom cupboard in Glen Iris. Then one of them said, 'We have some of the videos here.'

'I was shocked,' Josie went on, trembling as she remembered how shocked she'd been.

'I said to them, "This is personal. Why are you telling me all this?"'

He asked me, "Did he video you?" All of a sudden, I was worried, scared, very embarrassed. I'm a hot-blooded Italian girl in private. You put an Italian and a Greek into a bedroom together – oh! la! la!

'I was so embarrassed they might have seen the videos John had made of me. I thought I'd better be honest and tell them the truth.

'They asked me if I'd been drugged. *Drugged?* No! Why would I take drugs?'

'I've only ever smoked two half-joints in my life. I don't even drink,' she told them.

It became apparent the police had seen videos of Josie, so she was glad that she'd been honest with them. 'Your eyes are closed,' one of them said. 'Were you unconscious?'

'Unconscious?' With all these weird questions, Josie wasn't sure what was going on.

She leaned into the space between us. 'You tell me the truth, Robina, do you close your eyes when you make love?'

I didn't have to think for long, although her question surprised me back into my surroundings.

'I suppose I do, Josie. I think most women do, if it comes to that,' I said.

'*Exactly!* That's what I told them!' she said triumphantly. 'But they said there were other girls, drugged, unconscious, that the stuff they'd found at John's was not porn from the internet, it was his private collection.'

When police questioned John the day before, he'd told them, 'This is, like, a very, very bad time in my life. It just brings back bad memories for me.' He said that his victims were drunk or had been willing to take drugs. 'They were still awake, they was just lying on the bed with their eyes closed.' He said that some of the women had given him permission to do 'whatever you want'.

'They trusted me and they knew I wouldn't hurt them in any way,' he'd told the police.

Poor Josie. It was a pretty tough four hours for her. But the police had also been through a lot in the previous few days. Finding the video and DVD collection was only part of their job. Then they had to sit down and view some of the evidence before interviewing Xydias and

Josie. Watching unconscious girls being raped was no fun. It was rather like watching necrophilia. All part of the job, unfortunately.

After this, the action stepped up in both directions. As soon as she returned home, Josie rang John.

'We need to talk. Come over,' she told him.

When he arrived, he was defensive and angry. 'You gave them that DVD,' John said. He looked scared.

Josie was thrown off balance. The police had told her they wouldn't tell John she'd given them the change-room footage. But things had gone a lot further than that now.

'John, what's going on? Did you drink-spike those girls? Their eyes were shut. The police think they were stoned or drugged. *Tell me what's going on*!'

'Josie, promise me, promise me, we'll always stay together, until the death of me,' he pleaded.

Josie was taken aback. 'This was our favourite song, our song, he was saying,' she told me. *'Never Tear Us Apart*, like INXS, Michael Hutchence, you know,' she told me. I didn't know the song but urged her to keep talking.

'"What are you telling me?" I screamed at him,' she continued. 'I was scared. It felt like Armageddon or something. I was being pulled in two directions. I wanted to believe him, but the police had *evidence*. Him on a video. How can he get around that?'

John said, 'I can't tell you everything. The lawyers and police said not to.'

So, after tears and tantrums, Josie took him on trust – again.

While Josie was telling me her story, the phone rang. To my surprise, it was John Xydias, calling from prison! Josie spoke breathlessly into the phone and I went outside to stretch my legs. When I returned, they were still talking. 'He wants to talk to you,' she said. 'He knows who you are and that I'm telling you the story for a book.'

I took the phone, feeling a bit unprepared. I confirmed with him that I was interviewing Josie for a story and he said he was fine about that.

Not being able to think of much else to say, I handed the phone back.

After she hung up, Josie said we should go together to visit John. Have lunch out and make a day of it. I said I'd have to think about that.

By the time the local police had executed the search warrants at Xydias's two places of residence, they'd found a camera, tripod, photographs of women's genitals, women's underwear and tapes of Xydias having sex with women who appeared to be unconscious. They'd also seized bags and bags of videos and DVDs. At this point, they realised the case was too big for their resources, so they handed all the material over to the Sexual Crimes Squad, which was located in the St Kilda Road complex.

Detective Senior Constable Anthony Zagari was the lucky fellow who got the job of heading up the new investigation. Zagari had been with the Sexual Crimes Squad for about two and a half years. Previously he'd worked at the Asian Squad, the Drug Squad and as a divisional detective at Altona North. He'd been wearing plain clothes for about eight years, about half of his time in the job – an experienced officer by Victoria Police standards.

When he heard about John's case, Zagari hoped he might have inadvertently discovered the identity of the man known as the hot chocolate rapist, whom the police had been seeking for years. Up to 20 women had reported that a man had befriended them in Melbourne's CBD and the inner suburbs. He'd then offered them a lift and stopped somewhere to get a hot chocolate for each of them. The next thing they knew, they were groggy and he was raping them.

The hot chocolate rapist's last recorded attack was in 1998. After that, he disappeared from the radar. He hadn't been caught, unless he'd been sentenced to jail on a different charge, which is why serial offenders sometimes inexplicably stop. Or they die.

'I initially requested the cold case file of Hot Chocolate in relation to John Xydias,' Zagari told me, 'but it was clear due to his physical description that it was not him.' Furthermore, many of the women attacked by the hot chocolate rapist had reported the incidents, but it seemed that Xydias had led a blameless life until Josie discovered the video.

The police looked further into John Xydias's operation and narrowed down the instances of his alleged offences, which appeared to occur between 1991 and 2006.

Then began the difficult and distasteful job of going through the material they had seized. The seized footage was spread over kilometres of tapes and often disguised. In order to provide continuity and context, police had to copy the original material onto DVDs to preserve the evidence. Working with the DVDs attached to an electronic counter, they had to watch every centimetre of the recordings, consulting the counter to log the times, if possible the dates and, most difficult, the victims' identities.

The uninitiated might think that this could make for a good night in, Zagari said. 'Beer and chips and being paid to view a few off-colour movies with your mates. But not so. Most of the footage was quite sickening.

'Xydias was lucky he didn't kill any of those girls,' he told me. 'They were so deeply unconscious their heads were lolling, arms and bodies totally limp. They could have suffocated on their tongues.' Zagari and his crew dubbed Xydias the 'rag-doll rapist'. They realised the girls in the films were probably unaware of their situation. But the police needed to find them and inform them of a devastating situation of which they might have no recollection.

Police discovered that many of the alleged victims were women Xydias had met at work or through mutual friends. Many of them said they'd never been in a consenting sexual relationship with Xydias and had no idea they'd been assaulted until police contacted them. Zagari said the case was 'unique', in that not one of the alleged attacks had been reported before the discovery of the tapes.

The police got a break fairly early in their investigations. On one of his dates, Xydias took 'happy snaps' of the victim outside his family home in Dromana before drugging and raping her. Posing next to her car, the girl inadvertently helped police to find her, as her number plate was clearly visible.

In addition to his investigative work, Zagari took on a new role in victim liaison. His unenviable job was to break the news to the young lady in the photos with the car that the guy she'd had a good time with some months ago had spiked her drink and filmed himself raping her. Luckily for the police, the girl was also Greek, and the word spread like wildfire through the community of young Greek women that if you'd gone out with John Xydias, especially down to Dromana, you might just have a problem. The *Crimestoppers* line ran hot.

Not all the girls could be found so easily. There were eleven young women who police wanted to identify, and police believed they had isolated eighty-eight provable offences committed against them. Up to 225 charges were discussed, but 88 seemed like a nice, round number.

Zagari's job with pretty much all the victims was to show them selected parts of the videos they had no idea had been taken. They weren't shown the most graphic footage – just enough for them to identify themselves as the subjects of the filming and confirm that they had no recollection of the event. Some had been unable to recall hours, or even whole days, after being with Xydias at Dromana. One of the victims later told the court that watching the footage of Xydias raping her was the 'most horrific and terrifying moment of my life'.

Others later said they had lost their trust in people after being told of the assaults, some of which had occurred up to ten years earlier. Sitting and watching the films had been as bad as the physical trauma of the assault. It was as if they were being raped again while they watched.

Of the eighty-eight charges, forty-one concerned a former girlfriend of John's from the Greek community. Josie said she'd been in competition with this girl over John. Josie told me the girl had phoned her a couple of times and told her to 'stay away from my boyfriend'. When Josie asked where the girl had obtained her mobile number, she said she'd taken it from John's phone.

Undeterred, Josie told the woman to 'leave *my* boyfriend alone. He is going to marry me.' Josie told her that John had even bought her a ring.

John's former girlfriend hadn't known about the rapes until she was shown the footage. She became so sick when she saw how her boyfriend had assaulted her while she was unconscious that she had to stop watching the recordings.

'It was devastating for them,' Anthony Zagari told me. I got the impression it wasn't a walk in the park for him either. 'They were shocked, traumatised. It was like an outpouring of grief from most of them. Xydias had fed them cocktails of Xanax, Mogadon, Rohypnol, Valium and Stillnox – whatever he could get his hands on. These were all powerful drugs on their own, never mind mixed together. He placed the women in different positions and dressed them in his own collection of female underwear and accessories before raping them. Some of the underwear belonged to Josie,' Zagari said.

As well as investigating Xydias, police were interested in a close friend of his, Harry Barkas. The investigation went for about eight months. Zagari said, 'After that, we had the long job, a further six months, of putting together documents and the brief.' The long investigation required dedication and commitment from the police team and also reflected their patience and understanding in dealing with the victims. As you can imagine, police were anxious to have the matters before the court.

'To tell you the truth,' Zagari went on, 'I was shocked at how he'd committed these offences. Those girls were lucky to be alive.' Four of the victims are still unidentified, so perhaps they did die. Or maybe they can't bear the humiliation of coming forward. I tried to imagine what it would have been like to have the police knock at my door, asking about a former or even forgotten man I'd dated years before, and then telling me I might be a rape victim and asking me to come to the police station to watch a pornographic video to identify myself.

'Maybe it would have been better not to stir up all that pain?' I suggested to Zagari.

'Yeah, that was discussed,' he admitted. But I got the feeling it wasn't an option. This man was a serious offender and he had to be stopped before he killed someone.

The irony for Zagari was that after Xydias was arrested, police received many calls from women who identified his friend Harry Barkas as the hot chocolate rapist. Barkas, who worked for a doctor, had been stealing sample packs of sedatives and giving some of them to his good friend John Xydias.

'We think Barkas wasn't all that bright,' Zagari told me. 'He stole the drugs, which were not locked up, and probably swapped them for copies of Xydias's videos. He fantasised about filming sexual acts, but Xydias actually did it. Like some men swap footy stories after the weekend, we think these two swapped pornographic videos and drugs.'

Another irony was that Xydias used his football heroes to disguise his sexual perversions. 'You'd be watching a video which started off with the weekend footy,' Zagari told me, 'and suddenly these rag doll episodes appeared, inserted into the game.' No-one was sure if this was done to disguise the rape footage. Other Dromana footage was hidden in the middle of commercial pornography Xydias had downloaded from the internet.

Police took their time making sure their case was watertight. Meanwhile, Josie and John were waiting anxiously. Three months passed. Josie kept asking John, 'Have you heard anything from the police?' but he hadn't.

'Well, no news is good news,' she reassured him. 'So far, so good.'

But she'd begun to think that there were many things John wasn't telling her, 'because he didn't want to worry me'. Her faith in him continued, but she needed a break. In June 2007, she travelled alone to her favourite holiday destination – Phuket in Thailand.

'It was awful over there, Robina,' she told me. 'I got so sick. I think it was all the nervous worry over John. On the Monday after I got home, he came round to get the presents I'd bought him. It was a lovely night. We made love and it was just like the old times.'

She didn't see him on Tuesday, but on Wednesday night he rang and said a tooth was bothering him. 'He sounded strange, like his face might be swollen,' she said. 'Then I said, "Come over tomorrow instead." Usually on Thursdays I'd go down to Dromana, make it nice for him and we'd stay there. But with his tooth being bad, I said, "Well, just come over here instead." He said, "Hon, my face is all swollen. I can't talk on the phone. I don't know if I can come tomorrow. Who knows what will happen tomorrow?"'

It was a short call. Josie's antennae sensed something. 'I thought about those girls, the videos. I asked him, "What's going on?" He said, "Nothing is going on. Goodnight, hon, sweet dreams, I love you", and that was it.'

She worried most of the night. There was no word from him on Thursday or Friday.

'Next thing, on the Friday, my mum rang. She said, "Josie, I just heard a news flash on 3AW. John's been arrested. They say he's drugged and raped girls. I wanted to prepare you." "No! No!" I said to my mama. "Not John. He wouldn't!"'

She sat on the edge of her lounge chair waiting for the 6 pm news on Channel 9.

'Then on came Peter Hitchins, wearing a yellow tie. My favourite colour, like an omen,' she told me. 'I saw my boyfriend walking down some steps with three detectives. There were so many cameras! They got in this big silver car and drove off.

'I couldn't believe it. I started to scream, all by myself in the flat. I wish the police could have called me. They could have prepared me. But no. There he was on TV being arrested.

'I went into shock. It was the worst day of my life. Somehow, I made my way to my parents' place. I was crying, shaking. Then on Saturday afternoon, trying to get some sleep, I'm woken up at home by some journalist and photographer from the *Sunday Herald Sun*. I looked dreadful. He wanted a photo, so I found one of me and John.' The journalist took it.

She told the journalist how concerned she was for the victims and said she hoped they were getting the best possible care and support. The next day, a media throng assembled outside. Josie told them that she knew John had a picture of Naomi Robson, but she denied knowing that he'd allegedly stuck pictures of Robson's face on pictures of scantily clad women in suggestive poses. She said that she and John were still 'boyfriend and girlfriend' right up until she heard the news about the charges the previous day. She said she knew he saw other women during the times they broke up, but she had no idea of his double life.

Josie said that when they split up, he'd always go on the chat lines. 'We had many break-ups,' she said, 'but they were because I wanted to get married. I begged him and he wouldn't.'

John Xydias's parents also received a visit from the *Sunday Herald Sun*. This elderly couple had spent their whole lives working on their feet for fourteen hours a day to provide a good future for their only child. I couldn't imagine the kind of saving and sacrifice a blue-collar family would have to make to send their child to Wesley, which is one of the best and most expensive private boys' schools in Melbourne, and buy a house in a genteel suburb like Glen Iris and then a holiday house for their son and themselves. When they finally reached retirement age, they had no savings. They signed the Dromana house over to John.

John's father Nick told reporter Kelvin Healey, 'I don't believe this happened, but the police say that.' He described John as 'a very good son' and said he didn't understand the investigation.

'The police come here, [they have] got some problem with my son,' he said. 'Something happened, I am not sure.'

Nick said he was extremely concerned for John, who was in custody awaiting a court appearance the following day.

'If this happened to your son, you would worry about it,' he said. But he said he hadn't yet been able to discuss the allegations with his son. 'He went to the police station.'

After Josie's interview with the *Herald Sun*, a blog site used the photo she'd given the journalist on the internet. '*Without my permission!*' she told me.

The site was called NNN Reporters' Newsroom. It said that Josie, 'who dated Xydias for nine years, said she was still in shock ... after police charged her boyfriend with drugging and raping 16 women on film.' It also reported that she said she and John had stayed together in his parents' home and the beach house many times, and she never saw him rape anyone.

Josie, quite worked up by now, went on, 'They linked me with that creep Harry Barkas as well. The website paid me nothing for my photo and just assumed it was OK to plaster me and my John all over their blog. I wrote and told them what I thought of them.'

She did indeed. This is part of a much longer, furious post to the blog site, all written in capital letters:

> *WHO GAVE YOU PERMISSION TO PUT MY PHOTO OF JOHN XYDIAS AND I ONTO YOUR WEBSIGHT?*
>
> *I CAN UNDERSTAND IF YOU PUT THE PICS OF JOHN AND HARRY ON YOUR WEBSIGHT BUT TAKE MY PHOTO OF ME AND JOHN OFF YOUR SIGHT ... WHAT NEXT YOU ARE GOING TO PUT MY PHOTO OF ME AND JOHN IN "WHO WEEKLY" OR "PEOPLE" OR "FAMOUS MAGAZINE" OR HOW ABOUT "OK" MAGAZINE ...*
>
> *I DID NOT GIVE YOU PERMISSION TO USE MY PHOTO WHO GAVE YOU THE ORDER TO USE MY PHOTO??? AND YES IM PISSED OFF. I GOOGLE SEARCHED HARRY TONIGHT AND I SEE THIS RIGHT UP THE TOP ON THE SEARCH RESULTS OF HARRY BARKAS ... AND IF YOU DO NOT BELIEVE IT IS ME EMAILING YOU THEN TOUGH LUCK TO YOU!!!*

Her tirade attracted a lot of flak and no sympathy in the blog comments.

'God, what atrocious spelling and grammar! What the hell is your point anyway, that you don't like being associated with known criminals?'

'She turned the photo over to a newspaper. It's now in the public domain – anybody can link to it or otherwise tell people how to find it.'

This is pretty much the case. It used to be that if an unwise or uninitiated person spoke freely to a reporter, leading to a big story that shamed or embarrassed the person who had been its source, the story was only seen by people reading that particular paper unless it was picked up by other media outlets. Yesterday's story became today's fish and chip wrapping. Now, fish and chips are wrapped in clean, white paper and the downsides of baring your soul are endless thanks to the internet. Your photo can flash around the world in seconds. Copyright issues are still being debated. Defamation actions are costly and fraught with danger. A key witness in a case can view a suspect's arrest photo on the web, read a caption accusing him, and months later point to the same man in court and identify him as her attacker.

Josie was right to be angry and upset but she had no chance of undoing the contents of the blog. To their credit, though, the editors removed her photo, leaving a very sinister-looking John Xydias smiling into the lens. Josie became a bit of a media darling for a short period. She was courted by *A Current Affair* and tabloid-style media outlets, which offered her big money for exclusives, but eventually they decided that the subject wasn't suitable for their audiences.

Josie wasn't allowed to see or speak to John Xydias for nine months while he was on bail, because she was told the case was still under investigation. She expected her next embarrassment to be his trial. She decided to deal with that by not going to the court. She didn't want media photos outside the court and stories linking her with John to shame her parents any further.

As it turned out, there was no trial. Xydias pleaded guilty to twenty-five charges of rape and sixty-one charges of assault on eleven women between 1991 and 2006.

The next ordeal for Josie was attending the sentencing. She wore a dark dress with a big gold cross hanging from a string of pearl rosary beads. It was the first time she'd seen John in two years. It had taken that long for the legal process to grind to its conclusion while he waited in custody.

She sat behind him while his offences were read out, shocked and sobbing as he stood in the dock with his hands clasped and answered 'Guilty, Your Honour' as each charge was read out. Josie focused on his once-wild blonde hair, which was pulled back into a tight bun. Even though Xydias was dressed for court in a grey suit, white shirt and blue and white spotted tie, she was shocked at how he looked.

During the remarks made by Chief Justice Marilyn Warren, Josie nervously twisted her gold cross in her hands and whispered her rosary. Another of Xydias's victims was also there to bear witness to his punishment.

Justice Warren told Xydias his crimes were in the 'worst category', which always bodes ill for a short sentence. She said that the victims had been degraded and dehumanised by his actions.

She'd heard defence evidence from an experienced forensic psychiatrist, who had said that Xydias presented like a ten-year-old boy, inoffensive and humble, but in fact she found he was sinister and depraved and probably Australia's worst known sex offender. She sentenced Xydias to twenty-eight years in jail and ordered that he serve a minimum of twenty. At this, both Josie and the other victim present wept.

The victim said later that she felt she'd already been sentenced to life. Some of his victims might consider that he got off pretty lightly, considering that the maximum sentence for rape is twenty-five years per offence. If we passed cumulative sentences as US courts do, he might have copped a thousand years.

Chief Justice Warren said Xydias had shown little remorse for his crimes and still maintained that his victims had consented to the sexual acts. He had also denied drugging his victims, but Justice Warren found that the women had been rendered unconscious.

John Xydias was represented by veteran defence QC Remy van de Weil. I rang him to ask him what it was like, speaking generally, to defend someone who appears to be manifestly guilty. Mr van de Weil has been a QC since 1973 and has defended accused clients in many trials, so I thought he would have an opinion.

He told me, 'Our responsibility is to protect the rights of our client, even if he or she has confessed to us. If they plead not guilty, our role is to test the evidence and ensure the prosecution satisfies the burden of proof. Of course, we can't allow a client to give evidence if they have told us that they have committed the offence, so they can't be called.'

Mr van de Weil said that barristers are just like taxi-drivers. 'We get hailed by a client and we take them where they want to go. If they say they want to plead not guilty, it's like a customer telling the taxi driver to go to the Flemington racecourse. The driver might say, "No races on today, mate", but if they insist, that's where the driver takes them.'

Mr van de Weil's opinion of John Xydias differed from that of the chief justice. He said, 'John was just like a very polite, very charming ten-year-old. He was totally and completely immature.' Mr van de Weil thought that Harry Barkas, 'who is quite cunning, probably manipulated the situation between them, supplying him with drugs he'd stolen and goading him on to not only drug the girls, but film them as well. And John was so unsophisticated that he *kept the videos* – in his own bedroom!

'I don't think he is a monster. He's more like a bit of a drongo really, harmless and biddable, and he was totally out of his depth from the day his parents sent him to a private school. That school should never have taken their money. They should have told John's parents he was not suited to that level of education.'

We both agreed that the whole affair must have been a grave blow to Xydias's parents. They'd lost their only son so publicly and shamefully, and then the holiday house they scrimped to buy had to be sold to meet civil demands against John for damages by some of the girls. A tragic ending to a hard and frugal life.

Although Mr van de Weil did his best to demonstrate his client's lack of maturity and absence of sinister motives, the incriminating evidence against John Xydias was overwhelming on the day. The media had demonised him since his arrest by creating the image of a dangerous, sadistic rapist. The sentence reflected this widely held opinion.

Later, outside the court, Josie told TV reporters, 'He's wasted ten years of my life. Now he's going to waste twenty-eight years of his life.'

After the sentencing on 30 June 2009, Josie didn't hear from John for six months. Then one day in December he phoned her, and they began exchanging cards and letters. He sent her a romantic card and a dozen red roses on their twelfth 'anniversary'. She said she still loved him. She finally felt able to visit him in February 2010 and arranged to go again in early May.

But then he started baiting her on the phone. 'You lagged me, Josie. It's your fault I'm in here. If you didn't lag to police, I wouldn't be doing twenty years.' This totally unbalanced her. She told me it wasn't fair for him to accuse her.

'I did not dob John in for drugging those girls,' she told me. 'I decided when he said this a couple of times that he should recognise that he should have responsibility for his own actions. I'm still trying to understand why he did those things. I am still very hurt. I said to him, "Let's be honest, John, how about you? You're the one who filmed those girls. Lawfully, it was still rape. It's not a very good impression when you are there, on those discs – it's not a very good impression. If you didn't know they were unconscious, why did you try to open one of the girls' eyes?" John told me, "I was checking to see if she was OK. I was just going – Are you OK babe?"'

Josie told me, 'All I was trying to do was get the real story out of him. See his true colours. Then he said to me, "It's all about loyalty", trying to shift the blame onto me again. I said, "*Loyalty!* You want to talk about loyalty when you filmed those girls!? Why were you so stupid to keep all those discs? I was buying you *Christmas presents* and you were filming those girls."

'Then, Robina, he said, "I didn't know those tapes were there in my cupboard, I swear to God. I swear on my parents' life. I didn't know." I couldn't believe it. I wanted to say to him, "You look me in the eye – do you remember sex, drinking, dope? You are just full of *bullshit!* Now I see the real you," I told him, "It's over. I regret being in contact with you since you've been in there. Don't ring me. You're not worth my love and my support. You were the one who brought this on yourself. Don't you dare blame me for being in prison!"'

After this phone call, Josie rang the prison and told them to take her off Xydias's approved call list. Subsequently, she became a bit of a 'go-to' person for the media, doing interviews about anything to do with the case, or even vaguely connected with it. One media outlet planned for her to be interviewed with one of Barkas's victims. Some media have no limits in exploiting vulnerable people!

She was also approached by a man who claimed to lead an organisation called People Against Lenient Sentencing, but she became suspicious of his motives. He allegedly tried to collect media payments for Josie without her knowledge, pressured her mother to persuade her to donate $5000 to his group, and claimed he'd arranged for prison staff to tell Xydias that his pet cat – which died peacefully – had been strangled to death.

The man denied he or his organisation was attempting to profit from victims. He said he'd asked Josie for a $5000 donation in return for setting up a magazine deal and was angry when she only offered $1500. He also claimed that the only reason he'd arranged for a cheque to be made out to himself on Josie's behalf was that she hadn't wanted to give the media her contact details.

Josie denied this. 'I gave them my bank details on day one. He's a manipulator and an opportunist,' she said. There are a lot of sharks out there on the edges of the underworld!

In 2011, Harry Barkas died in jail, allegedly taking an overdose and sticking his head in a toilet bowl. 'You live by the sword, you die by the sword,' Josie said in a TV interview. 'No-one much would have shed a tear for him.'

She claimed Barkas was despised both in and out of prison. 'You've got to wonder whether someone got to him,' she said. She questioned why he would have killed himself when he only had months left to serve.

The coroner investigated the death of Harry Barkas, as she was obliged to do under the Coroner's Act, because he was 'a person placed in custody'. Barkas's family had also expressed concerns about the health care he'd received in prison. Having conducted an autopsy, Associate Professor David Ranson reported that Barkas had severe coronary atherosclerotic disease and 'would have been at very high risk of further ischaemic myocardial events and at high risk of sudden death associated with ischaemia related arhythmia'. The coroner decided against an inquest 'as it was not mandatory if the person was deemed to have died from natural causes'. Doesn't explain how his head got in the toilet, though.

Josie was now getting on with her life as best she could. She told me next week she was going on a date with a man she met on a telephone dating service ...

Postscript

It seemed things had turned out OK for Josie. She thought the man she'd met on the dating service was nice enough to marry, and she sent me an invitation to the wedding. I didn't go, but I wished her a happy life after the ten years wasted on Australia's worst serial rapist.

But this marriage didn't last either. At last sight, Josie and her ex-husband were still at loggerheads on social media. She was writing sad little posts about missing him and very personal explanations about why she thought he divorced her, along with accusations about their dog. She wrote in her trademark capitals, 'TE AMO MUITO MUITO POR SIEMPRE MEU AMOR!' Which means in Portuguese that she loves him very much for ever.

She hadn't given up on happily ever after, though. She was still searching for love, this time on a dating site for heavy metal enthusiasts. The last I heard of her was a sad little message on Facebook describing herself as 'a girl who belongs to no-one – I have nobody except for my Abyssinian cat and Japanese Spitz dog'.

Chapter Four

JUSTICE DELAYED

When I met Karen Keefe, she was in her early forties, a big woman, strong and tough. She'd been taking drugs in one form or another since she was fifteen. As a schoolgirl, she'd been lonely because she felt fat and plain. She envied the girls in the 'in' set, but she was never invited to go to their outings and parties. Then one night she was. She was over the moon to be invited at last.

That was the night she met Sharkey. He was twenty years older than her and was head of the Devil's Henchmen motorcycle gang, who were the biggest movers of illicit drugs in Tasmania and dealt in guns and ammunition as well. The relationship with him would be part of her life for the next thirty years. That night, he singled her out and introduced her to love, sex and drugs.

From then on, her life spiralled into chaos. She lied to her mother, stole from anyone she could get money from (including her mother), took and sold drugs and other contraband, and sometimes sold her body for sex. She'd hold up soft targets like late-night supermarkets, then return to the love and security she felt in Sharkey's arms.

She wasn't his only girl, but he always reassured her that she was his best girl. At the same time, she knew that competition from younger, thinner, prettier girls was always on the horizon, so she worked harder for Sharkey in his illicit dealings.

She fell pregnant but her relationship with Sharkey endured. She got almost clean from drugs during her pregnancy and felt wonderful after the baby girl arrived. Karen's mother and her new partner were besotted with their granddaughter and happy to look after her.

Karen's days were full of her daughter, but she was alone at night, feeling bloated with her post-pregnancy shape and grieving that Sharkey was out with younger, prettier girls. One night, when she was at home and miserable, Sharkey came by with a 'baggie', and Karen couldn't resist him or the drugs. She lay on her bed feeling blissful, with her baby on one arm and a needle in the other. After that, she gave up breastfeeding and went back on the drugs.

Soon after, she got a call from a bikie mate to tell her that Sharkey had been raided, busted and charged. There was no doubt he'd be going to prison. Karen frantically prepared herself for a raid, but it didn't come. Sharkey got two years.

While Sharkey was in jail, Karen was looking for love and found it in Reg*, who had a government job during the week and was a muso on weekends. He travelled a lot for work, and Karen trailed along behind him, in love again, leaving her daughter with her mother and her partner. Reg had another live-in girlfriend at home, but, having shared Sharkey for so long, Karen was undeterred. In any case, it wasn't long before she had Reg mostly to herself. Over the next twenty-one years, she and Reg had three children – two boys and a girl. But she hadn't cleaned up her act; her drug abuse continued in secret.

When she needed drugs, had a fight with Reg or needed money, she'd head off to see Sharkey. She bought and sold drugs and couriered money. She didn't arouse suspicion because she looked like an innocent young woman out for a drive.

One weekend she had to drive to Launceston to sell some drugs at a bikie hangout. She was in her late thirties and seven months pregnant with her youngest child. Seven members of a visiting interstate bikie club cornered her and gang raped her, one after the other, over nine hours. It was the worst thing that had ever happened to her.

They then put something sweet into her vagina and introduced a live snake. Snakes can't wriggle backwards; when the snake panicked and started trying to thrash its way out, Karen experienced the worst pain of her life. She told me it was excruciating and terrifying.

She finally escaped and drove back to Hobart, a three-hour drive away, then went to emergency. She spent three days in hospital. As a result, she told me, 'I'm not only scared of snakes, but also I have PTSD and I'm on the rape register. Not to be near any possible offenders.'

Luckily, the baby was unhurt, but the event scarred Karen like no other. She kept it secret for years, but finally confided in a prison counsellor at a time when she was suffering from drug withdrawal and post-traumatic stress. Her disclosure should have remained a secret, but it later transpired that police had found out about it. The details were soon known all over Hobart and police used the information to harass her.

◆ ◆ ◆

By June 2016, Karen had hit bottom. She'd been caught driving without a licence and sent to Hobart's Risdon jail to serve nine months, with a minimum of six.

Things would have been much worse for her if police had searched the boot of the car. She said, 'They told me to lock the car and leave it by the kerb. I went very quietly, shitting myself in case the cops searched the car, because I was on a delivery run for Sharkey. You don't need to know what was in the boot, but let's say I would still be in Risdon if the cops had found it all.'

Karen's mother, now single again, had stood by her through all the years of drugs, bikies, babies and lies. Now she took leave from her job as a child support worker to look after Karen's two youngest children, a boy aged three and a one-year-old girl, while Karen was in prison. Karen's older boy lived with Reg, and her eldest daughter was independent.

She'd hoped to continue her relationship with Reg when she got out of prison, but while she was in Risdon he married someone else and kept it secret from her. After twenty-one years and having three children together, it caused her a lot of grief when she found out he'd married another woman. Hoping she wouldn't lose him, she'd made him extravagant promises during her phone calls, which were recorded by Arunta, the prison recording system. These words were later used against her.

Over those years, she'd continued her covert relationship with Sharkey, mainly driven by her reliance on drugs. In prison, however, she had the opportunity to get clean, and she planned to see a lot less of him when she got out.

In any case, Sharkey was now living with a girl called Meaghan Vass. Meaghan had been homeless since she was a young teenager, and Karen had first met her when she'd come around to buy drugs. Meaghan Vass would soon become important in Karen's life for other reasons. She would become the second person in a drama triangle building around Karen.

If the network of relationships sounds complicated, it's because it *is* complicated. The underground in quaint little Hobart would rival the gangs of New York.

◆ ◆ ◆

It's now time to introduce the person who would complete the drama triangle. One of the inmates in Risdon was a woman in her early sixties called Sue Neill-Fraser, who was serving a 23-year sentence for the murder of her partner, Bob Chappell, on 26 January 2009. She'd been convicted with no body, no witnesses, no weapon, no cause of death, no motive and no confession.

Sue had an enormous influence on Karen, beginning while she was in prison and continuing after she served her time.

Sue had consistently protested her innocence, and inside the prison she'd become a strong, positive force. She became a mother figure for a lot of wayward girls who passed through Risdon. The women there loved her and respected her, and the guards treated her respectfully as well.

Karen credits Sue with turning her life around. Sue taught her to believe in herself and think of herself as someone, not nothing. As a convicted murderer and a lifer, Sue also had prison cred.

Unfortunately, at her trial Sue became the target of a very theatrical DPP, Tim Ellis QC; she was represented by a defence barrister, David Gunson QC, who didn't have the benefit of information from the DPP's office that could have given him a stronger alternative hypothesis to put to the jury; and the judge (who later became the Chief Justice of Tasmania) gave a summing up that adopted a murder scenario put forward by the DPP, mentioning eight times a wrench that the DPP had claimed was the murder weapon but hadn't produced. Sue's trial resulted in a unanimous guilty verdict.

The trial was splashed all over the Tasmanian papers each day, but it didn't cause much of a ripple on the mainland at the time, although Sue was scathingly described in one of the mainland media articles as 'a lady with pearls, a hyphenated name and splendid pictures of her favourite show ponies'. Descriptions like this coloured public attitudes about her before and during her trial. The same article went on to ridicule the 'proposition that the poor little "rich girl" got a bum steer from a sloppy legal system and unaccountably hostile police'. But that proposition was correct.

During the forensic examination of the alleged crime scene – Bob and Sue's boat, the *Four Winds*, which was moored in the Derwent offshore from Sandy Bay – the investigators used testing materials to create a saucer-sized swab on the deck near the gap in the railings through which people could access the boat. This swab contained a strong primary deposit of what they described as 'unidentified female DNA'.

Some months later, after Sue had been charged with murder and the DPP was preparing for her trial, Sharkey's girlfriend Meaghan Vass was arrested for shoplifting. A routine DNA swab was taken, which is done after all arrests in Tasmania, and it matched the swab from the boat. What had a young homeless girl been doing on the boat the night Bob Chappell disappeared? The question hit the media and was soon all over Hobart.

Suddenly in a tailspin, police consulted a forensics expert, Mr Grosser. Shane Sinnitt, a detective who was leading the investigation, said in a letter to Grosser, 'this girl is adamant she hasn't been on the yacht, so I am trying to work out the possibilities ... I am reluctant to believe her.'

Grosser replied, 'Given the strong DNA profile that we obtained from this swab, I'd suggest that this is indicative of the presence of a relatively large amount of DNA, which is more likely to come from bodily fluids, blood, saliva than a single touching event.' During Sue's trial, Grosser told the jury it was possible that Meaghan had 'spat ... urinated or something like that somewhere a policeman had trodden'. That is, she'd left a good sample of her DNA nearby, and a policeman had walked through it and carried it aboard on his boot.

It seemed a long shot. If a policeman had carried the DNA in on his boot, it would have continued to deposit in weakening concentrations with every second step he took. But the deposit found on the boat was the only one. It's at least as likely that Vass had vomited on board and someone cleaned up the mess. Rags that smelled bad and had a brownish colour were later discovered in a plastic bag in the boat, but they were never tested.

Other evidence was collected about this young woman. Witnesses may have seen her hanging around the area near where the boat was later slipped. Other witnesses emerged much later, saying she may have been seen with two men coming up the beach from a dinghy at Sandy Bay on the evening of 26 January 2009. (This wasn't fully communicated to the defence during the trial, although the DPP did call Meaghan as a witness.)

In early January 2009, Sue Neill-Fraser had recorded in her diary a break-in at the boat when it had been slipped at a location in Goodwood. If the burglars had been Meaghan and her friends, had they returned on the night of Australia Day?

What *is* known is that on 26 January 2009, Meaghan Vass was living at Mara House, a shelter in North Hobart, where permission was required to stay out all night. Failure to seek permission could result in expulsion. That night, she told the shelter management she intended to spend the night with friends at Mount Nelson. On checking the address she gave, Detective Sinnitt later discovered it didn't exist. When police asked why she'd lied and refused to make a statement, she said, 'I've just never been involved with anything this large before.'

As a minor, she had to have an adult present during interviews. Two appointments were made for her to come to the police station to provide a statement, but she didn't keep either of them. The police made no effort to find her and compel her to give an interview, although they now believed they were investigating a murder. How could her DNA have been deposited on the *Four Winds*?

Not having an original statement to work from creates procedural problems in a trial. Usually, a witness makes a statement, which then forms the basis of evidence elicited in court by the prosecutor, and then the defence explores any loopholes during cross-examination.

That part of Sue's trial went something like this. With no statement to work from, there was some argy-bargy between the DPP and the defence in the absence of the jury. Meaghan sat in the witness box, looking small, scared and frail. A couple of onlookers in court noticed a young man with a full face, short sandy hair, a receding hairline and bushy eyebrows slip in and sit at the back. His greenish eyes made contact with Meaghan's and never left her face. She began to shake.

With the jury absent, Ellis and Gunson tried to elicit some facts from Meaghan so they could properly examine her when the jury came back. She said she was living in Hobart in early 2009 and had never been aboard the *Four Winds*. She didn't remember if she went to Constitution Dock in January or February 2009, and she hadn't gone to Cleanlift Marine, another place where the boat was tied up. 'Never been there in my life,' she said.

Gunson asked a few questions. He established that she was 'pretty sure' that in January 2009 she was living at a Montrose women's shelter that she named as Annie Kenney House. She later said she was staying in a different shelter, which she described as a 'big block of white – a white complex in Lenah Valley'. It was clear she had no idea where she'd been staying on the night of Australia Day 2009. In fact, the police already knew she wasn't at either address that night and the place she'd said she was at didn't exist. This information wasn't shared with the defence before the trial.

When the jury returned, the DPP asked Meaghan a few general questions, then Gunson attempted to cross-examine.

'The police tried to interview you some time ago, didn't they? And you refused to be interviewed about anything to do with this case, didn't you?' Gunson asked.

'Yes.'

'Was there a reason why you refused to be interviewed?'

'Only because of the fact that this just intimidates me – I've never had to do or go through anything like this before, and that was the only reason.'

'You said you'd tell them nothing. It would've been easy to say to the police, "I've never been on board that yacht", wouldn't it?'

'Yes.'

Gunson took her to task for changing her story about where she was living in January 2009.

'Didn't you say a little while ago in this court that you were living in the Annie Kenny Montrose?'

'I can't really remember, sorry.'

Meaghan agreed with Gunson that the Montrose and Lenah Valley addresses were not the same, which was obvious. Gunson asked her again whether it was Lenah Valley or Montrose and she replied, 'I'm getting very confused and I have been homeless since I was thirteen, so it's very hard for me.'

Drugs can also do that to you.

Gunson pressed harder. He asked: 'It's not difficult, is it? You were asked the question in this court a few minutes ago?'

'Yes, I'm sorry.'

She confirmed, by saying 'yes', that she couldn't remember going to Constitution Dock around 27 January 2009. She agreed that it would be fair to say she'd never been to Cleanlift Marine in Goodwood. She agreed, by saying 'no', that she'd never been there in her life and that she was most definitely not there in late January or early February 2009.

After her cross-examination, Meaghan Vass was excused as a witness. She fled the court. The green-eyed young man was waiting for her.

Amazingly, she'd faced no questions from Ellis or Gunson about whether she'd been in the vicinity of Marieville Esplanade, Sandy Bay on 26 January 2009 or on any other day, or whether she had any knowledge about what happened on the boat on 26 January. There had also been no questions about her relationship with Sam Devine, the green-eyed young man in the courtroom, who was known to the police as being involved with stealing from boats. The jury wasn't allowed to hear this information, because the defence didn't find out about it until after Vass had given her evidence-in-chief, been cross-examined and excused.

The next day, Mr Gunson tried to recall Vass – 'in the interests of justice' – as he'd belatedly become aware that she hadn't accounted for her whereabouts that night and had provided the staff at the shelter with a fictitious address.

The prosecutor objected to Vass being recalled. He said that Mr Gunson only wanted to recall her for 'a bit more nasty badgering about where she was on what night', questions that he said were 'not only pointless, but totally unfair'.

Although Detective Sinnitt could have given evidence about the fictitious address without recalling Meaghan, the judge ruled that it was inadmissible hearsay. This ruling wasn't challenged by either counsel. In support of his application to recall Meaghan, Gunson said that he hadn't asked her about whether she'd been at Marieville Esplanade. He could have asked her when he cross-examined her the previous day, but he didn't.

◆ ◆ ◆

During an adjournment after Vass had escaped, a file was handed to Gunson, but it may not have been conveyed to the DPP, who was concentrating on the trial itself. This file would resurface in 2021 with explosive repercussions. It contained handwritten notes and emails sent by Detective Sinnitt to the Deputy Director of Prosecutions:

> From Detective Shane Sinnitt to ODPP lawyer Jack Shapiro and DPP Tim Ellis SC – Subject "SNF" Sent at 6.29 am on Tuesday 5 October 2010. [My emphasis.]

This email was sent *during* the trial, where another police officer, Detective Conroy, was giving his evidence-in-chief. The file contained Sinnitt's handwritten notes about the impossibility of establishing Meaghan Vass's whereabouts on that night.

It also described a phone call to police on 27 January 2010 from Peter Lorraine, a respected yachtsman from Sandy Bay, who said that about 5 pm the previous day he'd seen an elderly man on the *Four Winds*, which had a small dinghy attached to the stern, implying that Sue might still have been aboard. Lorraine undoubtedly did see a man, a yacht and a dinghy, but Sinnitt realised after that first interview that he was looking at another yacht, much closer to the shore. This information wasn't highlighted until September 2021, when Sue Neill-Fraser's legal team presented a detailed submission to the Attorney General.

The absence of this information during the trial prompted the DPP to base the case around Lorraine's incorrect testimony. Worse still, Gunson believed Lorraine over his own client, Sue, who maintained she wasn't there at that time. He even included Lorraine's evidence in his summing up to the jury.

The victims of this failure to disclose evidence weren't just Sue, the jury, the judge and the defence. In papers tabled in the Tasmanian parliament on 2 September 2021, Sue's legal team said, 'It appears from a study of the court transcript that Mr Ellis SC was also a victim.'

Sinnitt's notes of the phone interview didn't emerge until he gave evidence in August 2018 at a leave-to-appeal hearing, far too late for the jury to hear.

◆ ◆ ◆

During the adjournment, Gunson continued his attempts to have Meaghan recalled. He said, 'Given the level of DNA on the deck, that girl was on that boat at some stage. Now we need to be able to put that to her and see what she says about it.'

The new information would have allowed him to ask a more powerful set of questions of Meaghan. He could have asked her where she'd been and what she was doing that night. Having lied about her whereabouts could have compromised her credibility, creating a suspicion that maybe she and others *were* on the boat.

But Ellis opposed the application and the judge agreed. The jury had to make do with recalling Sinnitt, the detective who'd investigated her alibi. He offered no further details other than that she'd spent the night with her boyfriend, Sam Devine.

But had Sam been asked where he was? No. He hadn't even been interviewed by police at that stage. Sinnitt also failed to disclose his knowledge that Lorraine's information was incorrect, because he wasn't asked.

On recalling Meaghan Vass, the judge ruled:

> *The question is whether the possibility of her giving new evidence of any relevance would* warrant *her being recalled and the time and inconvenience* taken to get her back.
>
> *I'm very conscious of the fact that this is a murder trial and you can't have a more serious charge. But the question of just where Meaghan Vass was and what she did on the night of the*

> *26 January seems to be peripheral when her version of events is unshakably, or apparently unshakably, that she didn't go onto the Four Winds, that she didn't go to the slip yard in Goodwood, and that she didn't go to Constitution Dock at or about the time that the boat was there.*
>
> *In my view, the prospect of Meaghan Vass giving significant evidence if recalled is so slight as not to warrant the time taken to recall her ... So I won't ask the prosecutor to recall her, and I won't take steps to order her recall. [My emphasis.]*

This was one of the most bizarre rulings at the trial. If an exact match of a person's DNA is found at a crime scene, surely the court should make every effort to ascertain how it got there? Meaghan was an unreliable witness, but it was inexplicable that neither counsel had pinned her down and the judge had allowed her to fly away without recall.

Sue Neill-Fraser's trial and the amnesiac Meaghan Vass came into Karen Keefe's life while she was in Risdon. Karen and Sue became friends when Sue was six years into her sentence. She'd appealed her conviction in 2012, but her main ground – the presence of Meaghan Vass's DNA on the boat – was dismissed by the opposition as a 'red herring'. All she got from the appeal was a three-year reduction in her sentence, down to twenty-three years. This was cold comfort when she was sure she was innocent.

She then failed in an application to the federal High Court after the court was convinced that the DNA was likely to have been a secondary transfer.

Sue thought she'd reached the end of the road, but then the Tasmanian Attorney General, Vanessa Goodwin, introduced a new law awarding a statutory right to a second 'last chance' appeal. In this appeal, a single judge sits and hears an applicant's argument that there is 'fresh and compelling evidence' providing grounds on which to lodge the application. The judge then decides if the plaintiff can seek a new appeal.

South Australia was the first state to introduce the 'last chance' legislation, and Tasmania followed in November 2015.

Sue's legal team and her supporters – including prominent lawyers and film-maker Eve Ash, as well as several writers who were following the case – sprang into action. Even before the legislation was passed, feverish preparations for an appeal had begun. Acting for Sue in Hobart was Barbara Etter, a former CEO of the Tasmanian Integrity Commission who had resigned from that job and returned to legal practice. She found out that the foul-smelling rags on the *Four Winds* had never been tested. But at the leave-to-appeal hearing, a senior detective who worked on the investigation testified that he didn't know their whereabouts, so that avenue was blocked.

Barbara also revealed that the extensive glow seen in the *Four Winds* dinghy after luminol testing, which the DPP had suggested was blood from Bob Chappell's injuries, was either self-luminescence of the luminol, or a false positive, which can occur. But not blood. This turned out to be correct.

Another Hobart lawyer, Jeff Thompson, undertook to do some *pro bono* work to back up Barbara Etter. He went to visit one of the men mentioned as knowing about when Meaghan Vass had boarded the boat. The man in question was easy to find, because he was in prison serving time for assault. Jeff took in some photos to see if the prisoner could identify anyone who might have been on the *Four Winds*.

A Perth QC, Tom Percy, was signed on, as were Paul Galbally, a senior solicitor in Melbourne, and two Melbourne barristers, Chris Carr SC and Paul Smallwood, all *pro bono*. They made a formidable team.

The Sue Supporters group had grown stronger, and a play and a film had been added to the arsenal. The premiere showing of Eve Ash's documentary film *Shadow of Doubt* in July 2013 had also been the catalyst to assemble an outspoken coalition of citizens, lawyers, journalists, TV broadcasters, print media, authors, former detectives,

Sue's family and legal academics, just waiting for a chance to weigh in behind any new legislation. The film graphically demonstrated how mistakes by the investigators and prosecution had resulted in the accused having to prove her innocence, which is the reverse of the way the law is supposed to operate. The film went on to win several awards, but it seemed no-one batting for the prosecution saw it.

The play, *An Inconvenient Woman*, was written and produced in Tasmania but financed by a Canberra lawyer, Mark Blumer, who saw *Shadow of Doubt* and was moved to finance the theatre production to the tune of $120,000. He said, 'In my mind it combines my two great passions in life – theatre and justice.'

The play opened in Hobart with the looming possibility of an order for immediate closure. It premiered just as Sue's leave-to-appeal hearing got under way. The play's promotional material said, '*An Inconvenient Woman* does not make any judgement about Susan Neill-Fraser's guilt or innocence but asks probing questions about a judicial system under the spotlight.' It was an excellent production, and the timing was useful for interstate supporters, who got a double bang for their buck on the airfare, flying to Hobart to attend both the play and the hearing.

◆ ◆ ◆

While all this was going on, Sue was working with Karen in Risdon to improve her self-esteem. Karen responded to Sue's nurturing, and they became good friends.

'Back then, I didn't really read the papers much,' Karen told me. 'I had heard of Sue, of course – everyone had – but I thought she was just some money-hungry wife who bashed her old man over the head to get his money.' She soon began to think differently.

Karen said, 'We were in the same shared house, and I was in a bad way. I was suicidal – coming off drugs, leaving my little kids with Mum, causing her more hurt, scared Reg or Sharkey would find someone else. Six months is a long time.

'Sue was really good to me. She taught me I should respect myself for myself, not for other people. That I was someone, not nothing. Some nights, when I was really a mess, Sue would drag her mattress into my room and sleep on the floor beside me, holding my hand.

'She teaches stuff to the girls inside. I went to all her classes; I really wanted to get serious about learning and getting a qualification. She is just so amazingly positive. She made my time in jail bearable, teaching me to value myself, and gave me amazing support and guidance.'

Sue had established a large vegie garden, which grew all sorts of vegetables to supplement the prisoners' diet, and Karen helped her in the garden, planning defences against the marauding rabbits as they chatted.

During one of these chats, Sue's path and Karen's became irrevocably woven together.

Karen recalled, 'One day in the vegie garden we were just talking a bit about her case. She never discusses it inside the prison complex because she's paranoid about directional cameras that have voice recording on them.'

As well she should be, I thought.

Sue was waiting for her leave-to-appeal hearing, and she told Karen that the crucial issue in the appeal could hinge on explaining the presence of DNA from a young woman called Meaghan Vass, if she would just come out and give sworn evidence.

Karen said, 'Meaghan Vass? I know that girl. Why is she involved?'

Sue explained that Vass's claims about what happened the night Bob disappeared still hadn't been tested and said that someone had to account for Vass's DNA being found on the boat.

Karen said, 'I'll be getting out soon and I could go and find out what really happened. She's even stayed at my house when she's been couch surfing. I'll go and talk to her as soon as I get out.'

Karen was keen to repay Sue for her kindness during the previous few months. For her part, Sue was excited at the prospect that

Karen might be able to persuade Meaghan to tell the truth to her investigative team.

A couple of times after that initial vegie garden chat, Sue said things like, 'If you really can help me, I won't forget you if I get out of here. I'll look after you.' She even mentioned that she could help Karen to buy a house for herself and her kids.

Sue's like that. Lovely lady, but she talks too much! You have to be careful what you say anywhere in a prison. Even the corn has ears.

◆ ◆ ◆

Colin McLaren, a former Victorian police officer turned investigative writer, was working with film-maker Eve Ash to gather material for a television series about the case and also for a book he was planning. He was in phone contact with Sue, who excitedly told him about Karen's offer. He asked her to tell Karen to ring him, giving her a pseudonym to use, and he later came to visit her in Risdon.

He wrote a long report about that first meeting and his subsequent conversations with Karen for Eve Ash. The report eventually ended up in the hands of the Hobart police, because a lot of his documents on the case were later seized.

In that report, he said that Karen and Meaghan were long-time friends, and that Karen had told him Meaghan had left her diaries hidden at Karen's house.

Just before Karen was imprisoned, he said, 'Meaghan was in a fluster. Someone was asking questions about her involvement in the death of Bob Chappell.' McLaren went on, 'This may have been me, talking to Meaghan's mother, trying to coax her to talk.'

Karen had agreed to hide Meaghan's diaries for her, but soon after that, Karen went to prison. 'The day after Karen commenced her sentence,' McLaren wrote, 'her rented house was broken into and ransacked. Someone was searching for something, but nothing seems to have been taken.' Karen believed the intruder was Meaghan looking for her diaries.

They weren't found. Karen is good at hiding stuff.

Karen was now offering the diaries to McLaren to repay Sue for all her support, as she was 'the only innocent girl in there'.

The meeting was planned for soon after Karen's release from Risdon on 23 December 2016, a few weeks after the vegie garden chat.

McLaren wrote that Karen 'wants to meet up with Meaghan and see where her head is'. He planned to film the meeting but cautioned the film crew to be wary of Karen. 'She could be genuine ... or spinning a line.' He said he had 'set some tests to check her veracity' and set a deadline for when those tests were to be met. He cautioned all those involved not to let Sue know anything about his discussions with Karen. 'Under no circumstances' should any part of his report be communicated to Sue, he said. 'It would only spook her ... and would be wildfire in the hands of certain criminals.'

He also said that Karen had agreed to meet him in his hotel room when she was ready. This was a big mistake on Karen's part.

◆ ◆ ◆

While she was out of prison, Karen arranged to see Meaghan and meet with McLaren. She did both these things, but neither went well.

After Karen's release from prison just prior to Christmas 2016, she went to the Devil's Henchmen's clubhouse, where she knew Meaghan and Sharkey were likely to be found. Karen told me later that she, Sharkey and Meaghan had taken some drugs and were 'on a bed together and I said to Meaghan, "Tell me about this shit that you were on that old bloke's boat." It just poured out of her. She said she was terrified, people were hounding her, but she did say she was there.

'So I said to her, "Why not just come clean and tell them? There's a lovely lady, an *innocent woman*, in prison because of this!" She was crying and saying, "I know, I know. Not a day goes by that I don't think of her."

'I didn't put any pressure on her, I didn't need to. She was stoned, but I know she was telling the truth.'

Karen had also looked at Meaghan's diaries. McLaren reported, 'Karen read a passage of notes that related to the *Four Winds* yacht and the death of Bob Chappell. Meaghan wrote that she, Sam Devine and Paul Wroe stole a white and blue dinghy and went out to the *Four Winds* and went on board. Their intention was to break into it and steal what was valuable.' Karen told McLaren that Meaghan had done this several times, to get money for drugs and food. (Paul Wroe emphatically denies that he was the third person on the yacht. Sam Devine has also kept a very low profile.)

'They thought the yacht was empty, as they saw Sue Neill-Fraser leave the yacht in her dinghy. Once on board later that night, they were startled by Bob Chappell, who started yelling at them. [One of the men] killed Bob Chappell as Meaghan stood there watching.'

Meaghan's diaries confirmed what she'd said to Karen, so it was time to take things further.

◆ ◆ ◆

The plan was to meet with McLaren and tell him Meaghan had confirmed she'd been on the boat, then to try to set up a meeting between McLaren and Meaghan. Karen's meeting with McLaren took place in a fairly average Hobart hotel room. She took her two toddlers along, with a friend to help manage them while Karen was talking to McLaren.

Karen didn't realise that, hidden by a couch on the opposite side of the room, a camera was rolling, capturing all the hours of the meeting. Karen told me later the first time she knew she was being recorded was when she later saw the footage played in court.

McLaren disputes this and says she knew of the filming.

'Rubbish!' Karen said later. 'Do you really think I would have taken a two-year-old and a three-year-old with me if I knew he wanted to film me? I didn't want my kids on any film footage – no way!' Eventually, the little kids got bored and McLaren, obviously irritated by their presence, wound it up. Karen and her little entourage gratefully made their escape, without much of value having been filmed.

Fifty-eight days after her release from Risdon, she was bagged again for driving under the influence and sent back on remand. Looking back through my cynical eyes, I wonder if it was a police tactic to arrest her so they had her where they wanted her and had easy access to her. They didn't have to proceed with a rush to court, just keep her on toast on bail. And while Karen was in prison, someone raided her mother's house and took Meaghan's diaries away.

While she was out of prison, police and others would have had time to trawl through the Arunta recordings of her calls made in prison. They picked on conversations that they claimed showed that Sue was bribing Karen to get Meaghan to say she was on the *Four Winds*. My later perusal of relevant material sent anonymously, showed they had a great interest in Karen telling Reg, for example, that Sue would 'look after her'. She elaborated on this from time to time, and also mentioned to her mother she hoped to get some money when she was released. Sue had made some foolish but desperate comments, sometimes just in conversation. Sue saw herself in a helpless situation. Which she was.

Meanwhile, the pressure was cranking up on the two Hobart lawyers who had been attempting to assist Sue Neill-Fraser with her application for leave to appeal. Sue's extended legal team was outside Tasmania, beyond the clutches of the prosecution. But the two remaining in Hobart were just sitting ducks to be picked off and made examples of. Two more bits of flotsam in the growing vortex of collateral damage swirling round the Neill-Fraser case.

Barbara Etter was preparing much of Sue's case for the interstate team until the establishment pounced. In 2010, Justice Gregory Geason ordered her to produce her case file from a long-drawn-out, controversial coronial inquest (not related to Sue the Neill-Fraser case). The ruling effectively ordered her to hand over all her privileged communications with a client, gathered over many years, both hard copies and electronic files, legal documents and 'isn't it a lovely day' emails. Barbara refused on the ground of client confidentiality and legal privilege. Rather than comply with this order, she decided to leave her legal practice and relinquish her Tasmanian practising certificate.

At that time, she released a statement saying:

> Here in Tasmania it appears that there are too few checks and balances on the powers of the Legal Profession Board. I agree with the Board's counsel that their powers may be viewed as 'extreme'. I urge Parliament to take steps now to ensure that the proper checks and balances are imposed by amendments to the Legal Profession Act ... If that does not happen then other lawyers of integrity will be subject to the harrowing and stressful experience that I have had since 2014.

The legal establishment was still not content. Another lawyer complained that Barbara had commented while being interviewed during a *60 Minutes* interview that Tasmania Police forensic scientists had not discovered blood in the *Four Winds'* dinghy (which was true). The Legal Profession Board also brought another complaint against her, accusing her of making vexatious complaints. Rather than have the board investigate the complaints, her lawyer, Hugh Selby, said his client wanted all the complaints heard together by the Supreme Court.

After leaving the law, Barbara Etter has built a successful new career as an award-winning artist. Nevertheless, she had to put up with censure and ridicule from the members of her profession. She has also been kept 'on toast' since April 2019 relating to the charges being brought against her by the Legal Profession Board. These matters were finally brought to court for a directions hearing in July 2021 and were heard later that year. She was still waiting for the judgement in February 2022.

She and her husband sold their lovely house in a leafy suburb and moved to a big modern house in an outer suburb, as artists are not as well paid as lawyers. As a result of her leaving the profession, the Tasmanian community lost one of its champion campaigners against injustice, wrongful conviction, the infringement of civil liberties and inappropriate legal processes. Of course, this may have been the result some of those on the devilish island preferred.

Barbara and Hugh Selby have prepared a dossier (the Etter–Selby papers – see the further reading in this chapter) covering these and other previously unaired issues and emailed it to the attorney-general and others with skin in the game. The papers were tabled in parliament by Mike Gaffney MLC on 21 August 2021. There has been deafening silence from government representatives, as Hugh Selby expected, but no doubt the saga will continue.

For his part, Jeff Thompson, who was doing volunteer legal work to support Barbara Etter, was put under surveillance and then suddenly charged with attempting to pervert the course of justice. This is a serious charge for anyone, but it's career-ending for a lawyer. Police swooped on his home office and seized photos and material on his home computer, including notes he had made on the computer as an *aide memoire* after he visited a prisoner who was a key witness to the Australia Day activities. The police charge alleged he had interfered with the prisoner's identification of photos of a person of interest in the case. Jeff denied this. Police claimed to have evidence on videotape from the bugged prison legal visit room (very unorthodox to bug legal visits!) that Jeff had made suggestions to the man about his identification. As I said earlier, there are bugs everywhere in prison – not just on the corn.

Jeff appeared in court several times over the following months. He pleaded 'not guilty' when told he would be tried for deliberately influencing a witness to pervert justice. Each time he told the court that he hadn't any idea what this alleged breach of the law entailed, and he couldn't provide a defence until he was served with an indictment detailing the charges. Had he committed the crime he'd been charged with? No one knew, as he hadn't been given the indictment. He was sure he'd done nothing wrong.

Social media went haywire. One post rhetorically asked: 'Is this a case of perverting justice, or justice for perverts?' I was in Hobart for one of Jeff's court appearances on 23 July 2018. Representing himself, he seemed like a total innocent in criminal court procedure. He told the judge, 'I'm still no closer today than I was eleven months ago in preparing for this case. I am still waiting for the prosecutor to provide me with details of the charges and an indictment.'

Crown prosecutor Jackie Hartnett passed two typed pages along the bar table. She said the prosecution was doing all it could to progress the case, while still waiting for police to provide her with recordings of at least forty relevant phone calls.

Jeff said he couldn't proceed without that information either. He asked the judge to order the DPP to turn it over. The judge said that was not his role. Jeff should seek delivery from the DPP with a deadline. If the deadline was not met, the judge could order the DPP to comply with Jeff's request. *Good luck with that*, I thought!

But Jeff did finally have an indictment – it was on the two pages that Ms Hartnett had passed down the bar table. Jeff and I adjourned for a coffee to have a good look at it.

It didn't take long. The body of it was half a page saying that Jeff had a document on his computer which he 'could or would have used to pervert the course of justice'. He explained that was the *aide memoire* he'd written after his last visit to the prisoner.

'But did you share it with anyone?'

'No.'

'Send a draft report to anyone, or distribute information based on your private *aide memoire*?' I asked.

'No-one. I'd just written up what had happened during the visit so I wouldn't forget anything.'

'So you haven't *acted* to pervert justice at all?' I was trying to figure out the logic. 'Just kept good records for your own use?'

'That's right.'

'Surely a person can't be charged for what they *might* have done? I write little notes to myself all the time.' I showed him the black notebook I use for shorthand records of my court attendances.

'Look at this,' I said, turning to the notes I'd made during some evidence being given by a police officer. 'This cop is a prize arsehole!' I'd written across the top of a page.

In the wrong hands, that comment might be considered defamatory, but my private note, unpublished, mentioning no names, was fine. I dreaded to think what police would make of the documents on *my* computer!

Jeff's next hearing was scheduled for 15 October 2018. Surely Sue's case would be over by then? But it wasn't, and neither was Jeff's.

His case has twisted and turned through the legal system, with Jeff battling to obtain information about the charge/s against him and the police refusing to provide it. For example, he made an application under his Right to Information, which is what we mainlanders call Freedom of Information (FOI).

The police refused to comply, saying they'd seized about 10,000 pages of public and private material during the raid on Jeff's home, and they couldn't afford the staff commitment in time and money required to review it. (They estimated it would take 1167 hours to review 10,000 pages and would cost $107,916 at $90 an hour.) They said they'd have to review all the pages they'd seized to assess whether or not they were relevant to the prosecution case. They then refused under Section 19 of the Act, saying it was too onerous to comply. The ombudsman agreed and Jeff's application was rejected.

Jeff sought a review, so the ombudsman sent one of his senior Investigation and Review officers to meet the lead detective and have a look at the material, which consisted of two rooms full of paperwork and included an audit of the volume of digital files from police IT services. It soon became apparent that the police had vastly underestimated the amount of material they'd seized ('although not through any attempt to be misleading' the ombudsman said reassuringly); actually the volume of material to review was in the vicinity of 150,000 pages, which would take 17,500 hours and cost $1.5 million. The ombudsman probably gasped, and he refused Jeff's request a second time.

I was left wondering how all these thousands of extraneous pages were relevant if the charge was still, according to the indictment, 'intending to pervert the course of justice'? And if they were relevant, wouldn't the police have had to assess them all anyway before bringing charges? It seemed like a huge waste of police time and resources, which was pretty much how the ombudsman saw it.

Five years after Jeff was charged, he was still waiting to clear his name and finally have his day in court. The last word was that if the prosecutor had 'progressed it' to her satisfaction, a hearing was scheduled to begin in February 2022.

There was so much going on in Hobart that every time I sat at my computer or answered the phone it was like being sucked into another episode of *Days of Our Lives*. Meanwhile, poor Sue sat in jail, wondering whether she would ever get out, supported by the ever-growing activist group, Support Sue, which by now had attracted around 30,000 members from all over Australia. The Hobart legal system and its proponents were beginning to resemble something from *Gilbert and Sullivan*.

◆ ◆ ◆

When I was researching my book *Death on the Derwent*, I decided I should speak with Karen Keefe. She and Meaghan Vass seemed pivotal to the success or failure of Sue's forthcoming application.

After fifty-three days in prison, Karen had been bailed to live with her mother until her trial. She was already facing five gun-trafficking charges when, from out of nowhere, she was charged with perverting the course of justice. The police alleged that she'd forced Meaghan

Vass to sign a statutory declaration saying that she'd been on the *Four Winds* by threatening to 'put her in the boot' of the car if she didn't. Karen and Meaghan were becoming yet more victims of the collateral damage around Sue's case.

Karen's mother was living in a weatherboard house in a battlers' suburb, almost directly across the road from the Cleanlift shipyard where *Four Winds* had been moored during the court battles. Another coincidence: two important players in this story close enough to wave to each other!

I'd tried to visit Karen about a month earlier, but was greeted by fierce barks from a *very* big dog behind a two-metre fence festooned with notices saying 'Guard dog loose', 'Enter at your own risk' and so on. One sign was tied under a solar-powered light, providing no excuse for an errant visitor, day or night.

I'd learnt a bit of dog-whispering working with the Guide Dogs years ago, but I was concerned it might go straight over this dog's head or not be heard over the racket she was making, so I stood at the gate and called out '*Cooee!*' a couple of times.

My calls brought a woman who told me she was Karen's mother and was minding the little ones while Karen was at college finishing a hairdressing certificate. Karen had been drug-free for nearly two years, and she was trying to stay that way.

Her mother told me they'd had 'a lot of hassles', hence the big dog. They locked the dog in the back twice a day when the police came. I wasn't surprised. Karen wouldn't want to add assaulting a police officer to her charges!

'Why do the police come twice a day?' I asked.

'To check Karen's here, hasn't done a runner,' her mother said. 'And to let her know they're watching her.'

We spoke standing at the gate, being frozen by the wind coming off the snow on Mt Wellington. She didn't invite me in. She didn't seem too keen on writers. I resolved that a later visit on a Sunday would be the best bet.

So here I was, back again on a Sunday, with no appointment but fingers crossed that Karen would answer my 'cooee' and agree to talk. When I called out, a tall, strong-looking woman in black trackies and a black T-shirt with several visible tattoos came to the gate. 'Shush, Megs,' she told the dog. The dog stopped barking but didn't leave her side.

Karen guessed straight away who I was. At first, she didn't want to talk to me, having had problems after putting her trust in other writers, but we were both getting cold and she was in the middle of something important.

'You'd better come in,' she said. 'I'm in the middle of changing poopie bums.' Not a job to abandon halfway through. Megs positioned herself between Karen and me, and I walked in my best self-effacing way to the door, where the dog escort left us to continue her patrolling. An outside dog – thank goodness!

The lounge room seemed full of little children. Toys, beanbags, TV, noise added to the chaos. The child count was three, and there was a definite poopie-bum smell. Karen narrowed down the culprit, her toddler granddaughter, her oldest daughter's child. She laid the wriggling child on a beanbag and commenced the process. I made myself useful passing wipes. I used to be pretty good at this job when I had four kids under five.

Job done, we moved to the adjoining kitchen to chat, but the two youngest kids weren't having it. While Karen tried to make us a cup of tea, they were to and fro to Karen, into the fridge and giving me the once-over as well.

Lucy*, her granddaughter, was a cheeky little thing with an impish face and masses of wild, curly hair. Karen's youngest child, Ruby*, about three years old, was quieter. She was Lucy's disciple, following her everywhere. Karen's youngest son was absorbed in a game on his tablet. He hadn't moved from his beanbag in the lounge room.

'You look too young to be a grandmother,' I said to Karen.

'I'm 42,' she said. 'I have an older son and daughter, Mary*, who don't live here; I'm just minding Mary's daughter because she's working today.'

Karen was getting impatient with the kids interrupting. She said, 'Just leave us now, or I'll put you both in the boot!'

'What does that mean, Karen?' I asked. 'I've heard Meaghan saying that as if it's a dire threat. She now says she only made the *Four Winds* statement because you made that threat against her. *Is* it a dire threat?'

Karen laughed. 'It can be. Being put in a car boot can end you up out in the bush somewhere with a long walk home – or worse. But when I say it, it's just something that is common in prison, like, "You upset me one more time and I'll put you in the boot!"' She laughed again. 'It's an empty threat, because we don't have any cars in Risdon, but people say it all the time.'

The little girls were back again, so she put them both outside with the dog.

'Isn't the dog dangerous?' I asked nervously.

'Nah. She loves those kids. It's her job to protect them and she knows it.'

I was still a bit apprehensive, but at least the kids were occupied for a while. As long as they weren't eaten!

I had a lot of questions for Karen, but something told me she'd been questioned often and persistently, so I decided to let her set the agenda and tell me what she felt like saying. If that didn't answer my questions, I'd probably have enough rapport with her by then to ask a few.

Karen sat up on the bench opposite me and popped handfuls of M&Ms from a huge box. Her son obliviously tapped away at his game in the lounge, and endless verses of *Mary Had a Little Lamb* blared forth – a bizarre accompaniment to the information she was about to share about what happened to her when she tried to persuade Meaghan to tell the truth and support the legal push to get justice for Sue Neill-Fraser.

◆ ◆ ◆

'Sorry about the M&Ms,' she began. 'I live on these and soup and tea. I used to weigh 153 kilos, but I had a gastric band a few years ago, and it's all I can keep down.

'I haven't led a blameless life. I got on the drugs when I was fifteen, and for years I was selling what I could – myself, stolen stuff, drugs for my supplier and even guns and ammo. Nothing was off limits if I needed a fix. I was worthless, a piece of shit. On the rare occasions I wasn't shit-faced, I had no feeling of being a good person, just a nothing. You need to understand this, because it explains all this shit I'm in now.

'I started sleeping with Sharkey for drugs when I was fifteen and I fell hard for him as well. He had a lot of power as head of the Henchmen in those days, and people would leave you alone if you had his protection. Lots of girls were after him. He slept with a lot of them, sometimes more than one. Even though he bashes women, they hang around him. I've been bashed, shot in the arse and stabbed in the leg by various bastards, but that was my life back then.

'Adding to my feeling of being a nothing, I was huge, getting bigger all the time, eating rubbish and takeaway. Never cooked meals, just grabbed stuff on the run. The drugs mask your appetite, so you just eat anything to keep going. You'd hang around the clubhouse, get stoned, people would come and go. Nothing was permanent except getting the next hit.'

The turning point for Karen didn't come until she was forty, when she landed up in Risdon and met Sue Neill-Fraser, who steered her toward a more-positive approach.

When Sue told Karen that she needed Meaghan Vass to testify, Karen said, 'I told myself, "Here's this nice lady, *really* nice, she shouldn't be in here, and maybe I can help her. She'd been so good to me, and that was way before I told her I knew Meaghan."'

Sue said she had a friend called Colin McLaren, who 'had people who could hack into Meaghan's Facebook to find messages from and to me, so it was watertight that I really knew her'.

Sue believed Karen, she said, but they needed proof. Karen said, 'They did get in, and there were all these messages between me and Meaghan, which prove that we had a proper history.'

McLaren asked Karen to add him to her visitor list under an alias as her uncle, Mick Collins, with an address in Ascot Vale. 'That was actually his address,' Karen told me. 'I got Mary to check him out. The prison would have rung the phone number I put down and he would have said, "Yes, that's me."'

When a prisoner nominates a person for their phone list, the authorities call the person first, to make sure they are willing to accept calls from the inmate.

Karen went on, 'So, after trying a few times to get me to put him on my visitor list, Colin McLaren came in to see me. He used to phone me as well, using the name Mick Collins. The cops know all about him now. They've got Arunta of him.' Arunta, the prison phone-recording system, had captured all their calls.

'He came in two or three times. We used "aunty" as a code for Sue when we talked about her. They recorded *everything*, you know?' Karen still seemed surprised.

'Didn't you think they would?' I asked. 'There are "You are being recorded" signs everywhere, and it's said in a recorded message as the introduction of each outgoing phone call.'

'But not little me,' Karen said. 'I was nobody then. Why would they be interested in recording my calls?'

For someone so streetwise, Karen was pretty naïve.

She got out of prison in December 2016 and had Christmas with her mother and kids. Then she went in search of Meaghan Vass. She wasn't hard to find.

Karen said, 'One night I was at the Henchmen's clubhouse with Meaghan and Sharkey. Meaghan was off her face and there we were, all lying together on the bed. The Henchmen have these containers in the yard behind the clubhouse done out like bedsitters, and she was living there then.

'I said to her, "Tell me what happened on the boat, Meaghan." And she just blurted it out.'

'So what did she actually say?' I asked. I was dying to know, but a bit worried about interrupting the flow of Karen talking and munching.

'She said she, Sam and Paul Wroe found a dinghy on the beach and decided to go out to the big boat and nick a few things. They climbed on board, and Meaghan's still up top smoking – I reckon the DNA will be from her spitting, she always spits when she smokes, it's disgusting – and the old bloke came up, yelling, "What's going on?"

'Meaghan was terrified and wanted to get off the boat. She said she was making so much noise that Sam took her back to the shore, then went back to the yacht. She said she ran up the beach and couldn't remember what happened after that. But that was enough to say Sue wasn't there when Bob was still alive.'

Karen called Colin and told him where he could find Meaghan. Colin and Karen then persuaded Meaghan to make a statutory declaration of what had happened on the *Four Winds*. She confirmed that she was on *Four Winds* that night and Sue was not; that she was accompanied by two men; and there was a fight, a lot of blood and she vomited on the deck where her DNA was found.

McLaren was keen to have Karen provide extra support for Meaghan's evidence. Karen said, 'Colin flew me over to the mainland, and I had to put all that stuff about Meaghan in an affidavit. I went over there to recount the conversation I had with her.'

Karen said she couldn't do it by herself, so Colin also agreed to pay the fare of a man called Jason* whom she fancied at the time.

Karen told me, 'The trip was a bit of a nightmare, actually. I picked up my pre-paid Melbourne ticket at Hobart Airport; Colin met me and took me to a hotel in North Melbourne. We were supposed to see a lawyer in Essendon, I think, the next day. I needed a fix, and Colin stopped and got $300 out of an ATM in North Melbourne.

'I got really shit-faced that night, and Colin waited hours at the hotel the next day for me to get up. He was pretty pissed off. Finally, he got me out to the solicitor's office in Essendon, and they tried to read this affidavit to me that they'd done for me to sign. I fell asleep seven times! They kept waking me up to read more bits of it to me.'

Could someone who was still stoned and fell asleep seven times while reviewing an affidavit only a couple of pages long have the testamentary capacity to sign anything important?

Karen was still talking. 'Then I told Colin I needed to pay Jason $1500 as rent and bond to move into his place, so someone put $3000 into Jason's account, and we blew half of that on a good time. I bought my own ticket back to Hobart.'

She was proud of herself for having done the right thing by Sue. 'I thought then that I'd saved Sue, basically. I was her ticket out, because I knew the truth about Meaghan and I pointed them in her direction. Told Sharkey to keep eyes on her because she was important to me and my kids' future, because I believed Sue said she'd help me when she got out.

'I made a difference. I did something that was good. I did it because it was the right thing to do. I've never done anything right in my life. You know, like my mum's never been able to turn around and say, "I'm so proud of her because she made a difference." By helping Sue, I did nothing to lie, scam, scheme or bullshit my way through it. All I did was tell the truth and what was right.

'I remember one night in Risdon after talking to Mum on the phone, I was sitting talking to Sue and she said, "How's your mum?" She always used to ask me how Mum was. I said that every time I got off the phone to Mum, I felt bad. I said, "It's always something – the kids are driving her nuts, Mary's being bitchy, or the little kids are being naughty. I told her I'd never let her down and I did, big time."

'Sue said, "I'll never be able to thank her enough for bringing you to me." I thought she meant Mum somehow got me put in prison and I told her, "No, she definitely didn't put me in here, Sue. I did that all by myself!" Then Sue said she meant that Mum had raised a daughter with values and morals, and she owed my mum for that.

'She said, "You never would have helped me otherwise and I owe your mother that." She said, "You and your children will never want for anything else when I get out."

'I told her, "You don't have to do that. I never did it for money." Would it be nice? Sure. Who would turn it away? Who would turn their back on half a million dollars for a house? No-one. But I never did it for any money.

'Sue told me, "I'll never give you money, Karen. I'll buy you a house." She showed me pictures in the paper of houses on the Eastern Shore. Said her daughter Emma had been checking some out. I said to her, "They are all four and five hundred thousand dollars." I told her I wanted none of them. I said, "I don't need big houses, Sue. I need a little house with a big backyard, so I can have a sheep and where I can develop a nursery with a cafe. That's my dream. That's all I want."

'She told me there was no reason I couldn't have my dream, but that I should finish my education, stay out of Risdon and keep off the drugs. She said, "I'll never give you money, Karen. But the house will be in a trust for the kids." She was explaining to me that if she gave me money, I'd blow it on drugs.'

'Where did you think she would get that sort of money?' I asked.

'It was all from all these contracts and stuff that she had for her story. They showed me some of them. I'll show you some stuff.'

She went to find a folder of legal material, and I sidled over to peer out the window, to check on the little girls. They'd been awfully quiet since going outside. But they were playing away happily, with Megs stretched out in the shade nearby, watching over them.

Karen returned with some papers. 'Here, read this,' she said. It was a transcript of a recording made on one of those pesky directional camera recorders during a prison visit by Karen's mother, who had asked her exactly the same question I had: 'Where is the money coming from?' Karen had told her, 'Mum, I seen the paperwork. There's hundreds of millions of dollars.' She seemed convinced that the television coverage would bring in huge amounts of money. On a smaller scale, Sue's supporters had advertised a reward of $40,000 for evidence leading to her acquittal.

Karen's mother also asked, 'And if she does get you a house, how will it go if anything happens to you, with the kids and that?' Karen explained how she thought it would work:

> It will be a trust. It's the Education Department. A trust for the four of them. They've got $50,000 combined. Her daughter brought in the paperwork. It's not $25,000 for this kid and that kid, because obviously some will have greater needs. Like all this is really nice, but the only thing guaranteed is their education fund, 'cause that's the only thing her daughter is overseeing.

Karen and her mum spoke more about the situation during another visit on 29 June 2017. Karen was recorded saying:

> I will see this thing through with Sue to the end. And I would, even if there was no money involved in it. That woman does not deserve to be here, and nor should she be, but I'm not gonna let it take over my life. I'm trying to get everything I need done with that Sharkey … so I don't have nothin' to do with him when I'm out. I would like to see this through with Sue. Like, I've got so close to her in here, and she really is … She's like, you know, the nights I wanted to kill myself, she stayed awake on her mattress on the floor, so I didn't have to be alone. Well before the Meaghan thing. She really is my friend and she's a decent friend. She wants nothing from me, you know – of course, yes, she wants me to follow through, make sure Meaghan doesn't withdraw …

Karen's mum said she feared for Karen's safety. 'Don't you think they'll get you? Someone will get you and kill you when you get out?' Karen was defiant. 'Let 'em do what they want,' she said.

But it turned out that what they wanted wasn't what she'd been expecting.

◆ ◆ ◆

In May 2017, Robert Richter, an eminent Victorian QC, came to Hobart and presented the premier, Will Hodgman, with a dossier of material relating to Sue Neill-Fraser's case. The dossier included an extract from Meaghan Vass's statutory declaration saying that she and two men had been on the yacht the night Bob Chappell disappeared. Richter left a copy of the dossier with the solicitor-general, Michael O'Farrell SC, with a request that he keep the information secret – and, in particular, that he not share it with the Tasmanian police.

Richter went back to Melbourne and waited for a response. But when the reaction came in August, it wasn't what he expected. The dossier had been given to police, who had set out to hunt down the sources of the new information. Rather than reappraising the case or reviewing the evidence, police used the dossier as a weapon to intimidate anyone involved in eliciting Meaghan's statement that she had been on the yacht.

When going through the Arunta recordings of Karen's phone calls, police had fastened on the notion that Karen had attempted to influence Meaghan because she was hoping to make money out of Sue's release. They homed in on Karen's exaggerated claims about the money she stood to make from securing Meaghan's cooperation.

Karen told me that when she spoke to Sharkey or Reg on the phone from prison, she made up all sorts of amounts of money, contracts, agents – anything to keep them both on a string. She exaggerated because she was scared that Sharkey and Reg would desert her while she was in prison, with Sharkey transferring his affections to Meaghan and Reg to anyone but her. 'Money talks with those guys,' Karen told me. Sadly for Karen, both things came to pass.

'I would have had nobody if they'd left me,' Karen told me. 'I was just trying to keep them both with me.'

Much later, I saw the Arunta transcripts of some of those calls, and Karen was certainly exaggerating the financial benefits she would get for helping Sue.

Sue's daughter Sarah has said that Karen's claims about Sue promising her financial assistance are false. I also asked Sue about it during a prison visit, and she couldn't remember such extravagant promises.

Listening to Karen, I knew I'd need time to absorb the afternoon's revelations, to think everything through in view of what I knew from other sources. Being trusted with someone's private pain and anxiety often puts me in a difficult spot. People I interview always know I'm writing a book, but I sometimes think they don't have that front of mind when sharing very personal information. I have to judge what goes in and what's best left unsaid. An ethical struggle of my own, at times.

Karen had told me she didn't want her life story 'splashed all over the media. I don't want to cause my family any more humiliation'. But to set some records straight, she agreed to open her heart to me. Now I had to figure out how to use that material, if at all. She'd become caught up in a case that had caused a lot of collateral damage and potentially placed her in danger. She could get bashed, or put in the boot of a car!

I was also concerned that my film-maker friend Eve had been put in harm's way. In one recorded conversation, Karen had described Eve as 'the one with the money, overseeing it all'. If police took this literally, Eve would become a person of interest (if she wasn't already). She had already figured they were trying to get something on her, but did Karen's uninformed view of her role exacerbate that situation?

Colin McLaren was a different proposition. Tasmanian police were branding him a private investigator operating without a current licence, which he denied. I'd known about him for years – former cop, writer, film-maker; he's done a lot in his life and written several books about his exploits. He was tough enough to look after himself.

In the Arunta transcripts I saw later, his phone conversations with Karen were headed 'Mack COLLINS (McLaren)', so he was fooling nobody. His visit to her on 28 November 2016 posing as 'Uncle Mick' was definitely recorded.

Several attempts I've made to speak to Colin McLaren were thwarted. It seemed he was keeping a low profile.

Karen told me that her hero-worship of McLaren had turned to ashes after she finally twigged that he'd been using her, and that the world cruise he'd offered her would never happen.

I was standing up to leave when Karen said she wanted to tell me something else. Hoping I was still able to take more in, I sat down again.

◆ ◆ ◆

Karen said she was in a singlet and pyjama pants, wiping down the kitchen benches in the Risdon prison house she shared with Sue, when the guards pounced. It was the morning of Tuesday 8 August 2017. 'They told me to get my prison garb and put it on, then marched me off, without telling me why, or what, or anything. They put me in the "tank" – it's a glass cubicle to allow guards to watch over suicide risks. I kept asking the guards what was going on, but they wouldn't tell me anything, only that they were not allowed to talk to me.

'After a while, some guards got me out of there and put me in a paddy wagon. No-one would say why. Bear in mind, I was already serving a prison sentence in minimum. I was racking my brains to try to work out what I'd done to deserve this treatment.

'I was taken to the Hobart remand centre, now called the reception centre, and shoved in a cell. The reception centre is a maximum-security unit. I had already been through the classification process and designated as serving my sentence in minimum. Shouldn't have been there. No-one was allowed to talk to me. I asked to ring my lawyer, or my mum, who was in Queensland on holiday with the kids. No go.'

The Hobart Reception Centre accepts charged felons before their legal proceedings and after they are convicted, pending their classification and placement at other correctional centres in Tasmania. It's a temporary high-security holding centre. There doesn't seem to be any protocol for holding sentenced prisoners who've already been classified, especially in solitary confinement.

'Nobody would tell me what was going on. Why I was there? I needed my meds. I needed my therapeutics', by which Karen meant her prison counsellor. 'I needed to talk to my mum or my lawyer. I only had a supervised half-hour walk in the yards once a day. They brought me sandwiches to eat and I told them because of my lap band I couldn't eat sandwiches, only soup. They kept bringing sandwiches and I kept sending them back.

'I asked for a shower. Not allowed. On the third day, I got my period. I demanded a shower and change of clothes, so they took me down the hall to the bathroom. I looked around me and realised I was on an all-male floor. As a registered victim of male assault, I'm not supposed to be kept in close proximity with potentially violent males. I asked them to shut the bathroom door for privacy. All they did was drag a table across the open-door gap, and I had to shower with no privacy.'

It wasn't exactly an ethical way to treat someone with PTSD either.

'After about three days of this, someone came to take me to the Hobart police station, which is next door to the remand centre. I was put in an interview room with two police officers on the other side of the table and banks of recording gear.'

One of the police interviewing her was Shane Sinnitt, who had been involved with Sue Neill-Fraser's case from the outset, and the other was a detective by the name of Jamie Hart. 'There were photos of my kids, downloaded from Facebook, face up on the table. One of the cops leaned over and turned the photos face-down. He said that unless I co-operated with them, it could be ten years before I saw my kids again. The cop said I was facing serious charges.'

Karen later found out that police had also told Reg that she might do six years on the charges they had against her, which may have been one reason he decided to marry someone else.

The police asked her about her conversations regarding the money she was expecting for identifying Meaghan Vass. She told the police,

'Look, everyone was talking about Meaghan and the reward, and her being the one on the boat, and I'm the only fuckhead that talked about it on the phone, obviously. Everyone was trying to get to Meaghan first. I didn't realise that they already had her name matched with the DNA on the boat.'

She told me, 'And between the two jail sentences, I've had a shift in me. Like, then I could lie through my teeth. Didn't matter who to, didn't matter what. I'd lost Mary – she wanted nothing to do with me. She's got my granddaughter and I'd lost her. Like, I was nothing to her. I sold drugs. I was nothing. I wanted her to love me.

'Money talks to my kid. Like Reg, who raised her, she is money-oriented. If I could just keep him hanging on to see that I was changing, to see that I was gonna be all right. But between now and then, it's not the same.

'I couldn't care two fucks for the money now, but back then was I motivated by it? I was a drug addict. Of course I was! Did I force Meaghan into it? No. Did I lose control of it? Yes. Did I make myself a bigger player than I really was? Yes. Don't take any notice of my Aruntas. They're fucked.'

The police told her they could only go on what had been recorded and what's been transcribed.

And so it continued for six hours, with two toilet breaks and two bottles of cola on an already empty stomach. As Karen stood to leave, she reached for one of the children's photos, but a detective took it out of her hand. He said, 'You don't get that until we get what we want.'

Finally, Karen returned to her cell, after being told she'd be charged with perverting the course of justice for her role in the Meaghan Vass episode. When she tried to complain about her treatment after the recordings had been turned off, Karen told me one of the police said, 'We don't care if Neill-Fraser is innocent or not. If she gets out, it will cost the state $120 million. We don't care about you either. You are just collateral damage.'

Karen's solitary confinement continued. She'd still not been able to speak to her mother or her lawyer. After three more days, she asked to see the police interviewers again. She thought that perhaps there were some areas she might clear up and that then she could go back to Risdon.

That interview covered the same ground for three hours. She didn't withdraw her story. She refused to plead guilty to the charges regarding Meaghan. As she left to go back to her cell, one of the police said casually, 'Still scared of snakes, Karen?'

'That totally freaked me out,' she told me. 'I'd only told one person in the prison system about the Launceston assault, and that was my prison counsellor. When the snakes were mentioned, I felt like everything was against me. He'd seen my whole private file – like everyone was using me as a nothing, just to suit their own needs in this crazy case.'

Her second interview hadn't done her any favours, because she wouldn't say she was guilty of anything other than trying to do the right thing. She was told she'd be transferred to Launceston, three hours' drive from everyone she loved. Sure enough, after a weekend that dragged through the lonely hours, she was taken in the prison transport to Launceston Remand Centre.

The boss of the centre, Geraldine Hayes, known among inmates as the 'Dreaded Geraldine', was on hand when Karen arrived. Karen told me, 'She wasn't so bad, but I was still not allowed to make a phone call. I was getting hysterical about my situation. Nobody knew where I was. For a week I hadn't spoken to a doctor, my lawyer, no support people at all. I was hungry, in the middle of my period, and confused.'

She told me a kind warder finally felt sorry for her, slipped her a mobile phone, turned their back, and said, 'You've got two minutes.' She rang her lawyer, who luckily was in. 'Help me!' she begged.

The lawyer rang Launceston, but the remand centre initially denied all knowledge of Karen. 'I know she's there,' the lawyer said. 'I just spoke to her on the phone. I want her released immediately.'

Karen was returned to Risdon, but to a cell, not the shared house with Sue. Her lawyer said, 'Don't speak to Sue again. You are in a lot of trouble.' No further calls came from Colin or his alias either.

I must have been looking a bit pale by then, so Karen suggested I take something with me to look over in my own time. She gave me some handwritten pages and waved me goodbye, surrounded by clinging kids and a big, soppy dog.

◆ ◆ ◆

As I drove back to town, I tried to put some order into Karen's story. Was it all true? She'd readily admitted she was a good liar. She's no pushover and she's run with some of the top echelon of the Hobart underworld over the years. But she was also a young woman trying hard to get her life on track, be a good mother and daughter, and stay off the drugs. There was something genuine about her acceptance of me and the trust she'd shown to tell her story.

I believed her.

Karen's pages were what the legal system calls 'contemporaneous notes'. They were documentary evidence of what she did, said, observed, and was told, written as the events took place, or as soon after as practical. These kinds of notes are used as records of actions during an incident or investigation. They can also provide details and accountability long after your memory has faded. They're accepted as evidence in courts of law.

Here are Karen's contemporaneous notes.

Tuesday 8/8/17

Lock down from 10 am. Walk late arvo. No phone calls, but Shaun W* [the facility manager] will come and see me in the morning.

No phone calls. No explanation. Nobody seemed to be allowed to talk to me. Asked for therapies – they said tomorrow. Lunch – sandwiches and soup. Ate soup, didn't stay down. Slept in clothes although I was allowed a shower. Normal meds. Begging to call my mum – NO.

Constable Joe D'Alo shaking hands with Chief Commissioner Mick Miller after graduating from the police academy
Albi Paris

Police searching the house of a suspect in the Silk–Miller murder case
Nicole Garmston / Newspix

Joe D'Alo in his new role as a builder
Deborah Varney

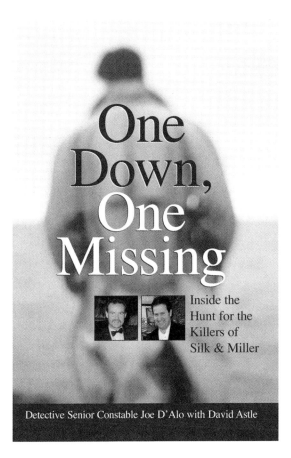

The book that ended Joe D'Alo's police career
Reproduced with permission from Hardie Grant

Memorial plaque for Gary Silk and Rodney Miller
Reproduced with permission

Roberta Williams leaves a hairdressers in Essendon, 2010
Jon Hargest / Newspix

Judy Moran outside the Supreme Court, 2009
Michael Potter / Newspix

Zarah Garde-Wilson leaves the Melbourne Magistrates' Court, 2005
Shannon Morris / Newspix

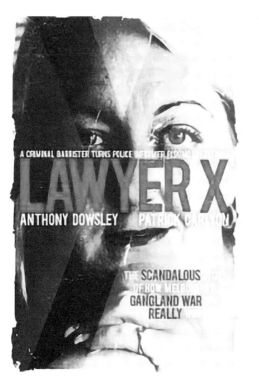

The explosive book
exposing 'Lawyer X' as
lawyer Nicola Gobbo
*Reproduced with permission
from HarperCollins*

Danielle Maguire and Renate Mokbel arriving at the Supreme Court in
Melbourne, Victoria
Kelly Barnes / Newspix

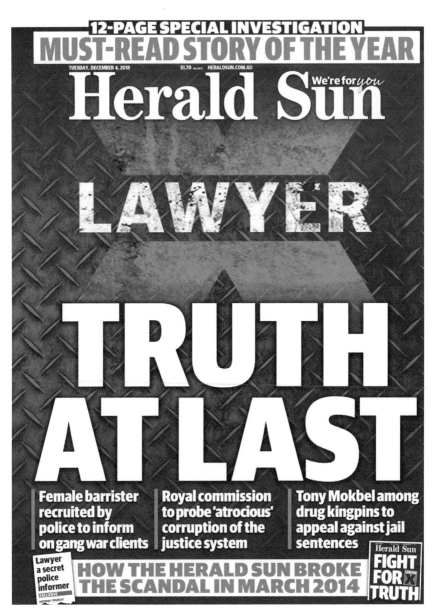

The front page of the Herald Sun, 4 December 2018

News Limited / Newspix

John Xydias
David Geraghty /
Newspix

Josie, alone again
Robert Leeson /
Newspix

Karen Keefe and her mother outside the Supreme Court after police dropped all perverting justice charges against her
Reproduced with permission/Karen Keefe

Meaghan Vass, Bob Chappell and the *Four Winds*
Photo courtesy of 60 Minutes

The Hobart *Mercury*
cover that terrified
Meaghan
*Reproduced with
permission from
the Hobart* Mercury

Mr Robert Richter QC, a strong supporter of the innocence of Sue Neill-Fraser, says that the case has been riddled with inaccuracies and enormous flaws, including ignoring key evidence.
Photo courtesy of 60 Minutes

CityGirl Han
22 Feb 2020 · 👥

Caught up with my brother today, love him to bits xxx

Noel Han and his sister Leonie
Reproduced with permission

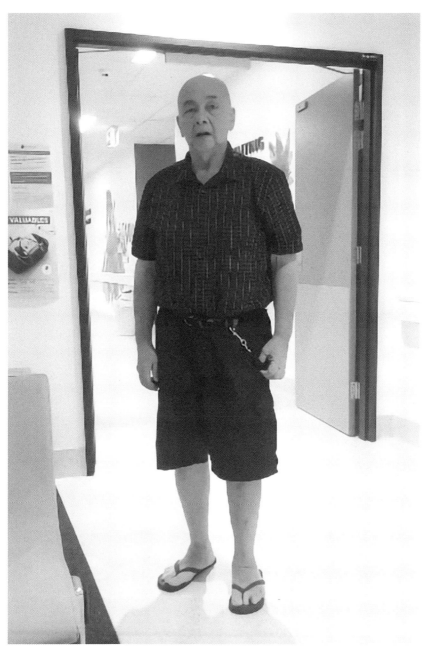

Noel Han leaving hospital after treatment
Reproduced with permission

Louie Bengoa on a police walk-around
Police photograph, court exhibit

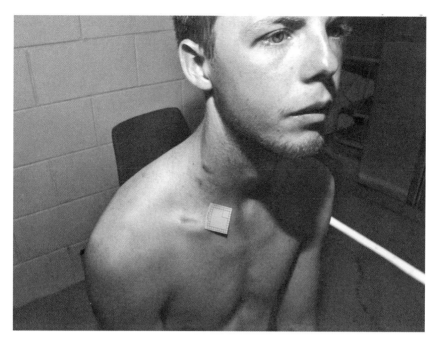

Dean Webber showing his injuries on the night
Police photograph, court exhibit

Dean Webber taking police on a walk-through of 2 Topton Street
Police photograph, court exhibit

Retired detective Gavin Neal, who led the investigation into the Alva
Beach stabbings

Reproduced with permission

Wednesday 9/8/17

Barely slept. Normal meds and valium. Still downstairs. Still asking to talk to Mum. No-one still knows anything. They keep saying Mr W will come see me. Nothing yet. Weetbix, no. Nothing but Milo is staying down. Two detectives take me with a warder – It's about Sue. They question me for nearly six hours with a couple of toilet breaks included.

2 x cans of Coke + chocolate. I told the truth. They weren't happy. They charged me. Return me to cells. Spoke to Adam [a police officer who knew Karen well]. Talked to therapeutics – Richard.

Thursday 10/8/17

Charged. Pervert course. False statement – Witness interfering. New lawyer, Damien or Daniel. Back to court 24/8/17. Still no Mr W. Blitzed tea – nope, ice-cream – nope, Milo – yep. Normal meds. Allowed to call Mum. Media is all negative.

20 minutes outside. Got some of my own things today. Photo of kids. God, I love them. Asked for therapeutics – nope, although officers said I could see Richard. I didn't.

Friday 11/8/17

NO sleep again. 8.30 weetbix – nope, Milo – yep. Still no Shaun W. Still 23.5 hr lockdown. Adam came had a chat. He will call mum and Mary. Cleaned my little cell.

Asked to see Sinnitt and Hart again. Told them everything I can remember. Another 3.5 hours interview. Canteen came. Video link with therapeutics. Try to sort meds. Apparently here till Monday. Adam says Mary wants to see me. 3.45 went walking for half an hour. Got some books. Met Mr W in the lift. He said I can call mum and Mary. Meds 30 metazapine. Thank God. Staff have been awesome but I'm going crazy. I can't eat the food.

Saturday 12/8/17

Was a mild night for a Friday. Not too much in the way of loud unruly drunks. Some girl calling out to me. I didn't answer. No need. I don't think anyone has anything nice to say to me. Started reading a new book. Peter Robinson *Children of the Revolution*. It's OK. A DCI Banks novel. It's very isolating and lonely here. I'm wondering if Sue hates me. Will she believe the bullshit in the media? Or the truth? Which she already knows. I'm so confused about everything. What's real and what's not. Did she do it? No, I don't think so. Meaghan definitely has something to hide. She is scared and not telling the whole truth. And now that she's been tracked, I'm gonna suffer. I just dunno what to do, where to turn, who to trust ... Last night was probably the most sleep I've had all week. I was exhausted and double metazapine would have helped. Think I ate all my M&Ms. LoL. 2.30 had a shower/bath. Asked for therapeutics again. 3.45 pm still haven't been for a walk. I'm going crazy. I feel empty. Like a zombie. Caged animal. Crying all the time. 3.45 went for a walk about 20 mins. Changed my books. I feel like an animal. Although I've asked for therapeutics – nothing. Just give me meds for fuck sake.

Sunday

Andrew the psych came to see me. I think even he felt I'd been railroaded. They did pre-warn me I'd be going to Launceston to live for a while. WTF?

Monday

Launceston – Wasn't such a bad trip up. But it fucking sux here. Hullo Hell. I've met the dreaded Geraldine. I don't think she's the dragon lady they say. She was nice enough to me. Said she will see me Wednesday. This isn't set up for women at all. Can't even see daylight. Concrete. Concrete. Concrete!! And it's filthy. I've washed my cell. It's fuckin' putrid, and all men!!! OMFG. How on earth will I cope? I'll need therapeutics more than regularly. Rang mum, talked to kids. God I love them. 4.15 Guards call lockdown!! WTF? I had no idea. I thought she said I could wander in and out. I'm fucking minimum for Christs sake. Chicken and veg for tea. Blitzed my vegies. It's perfect – as perfect as this shit gets. Apparently they've charged someone else. Who's that, I wonder. Will have to watch the news. [That was Jeff Thompson.]

Tuesday

I keep asking for therapeutics. I hate it here. Although it's better than HRP [Hobart remand]. It's cold. It's loud. And some of the officers are just maggots. Some are nice. I've been trying to sort puzzles most of the day. Had soup for lunch. Did a little exercise, but mostly did the 3250-piece jigsaw. Mum comes home today. God I hope the house is OK. Talked to Mary. At least she's in good spirits. I asked her for some phone money.

Wednesday

Should be canteen day. ARGHHH. Couldn't eat breakfast. Weetbix. Asked for clothes. Got two size 8 jumpers and a T-shirt. WTF? [Karen is about a size 16]. Still no therapeutics. I'm certain I'm losing my mind. Spoke to mum. Got a new lawyer from Legal Aid.

Karen's notes finish here, but she told me the end of the story. The experience cowed and shattered her. The mention of the snake, the photos of her kids, and, worst of all, being told she was 'collateral damage' gave her nightmares. Later, looking through the hundreds of pages of transcripts of interviews, I couldn't find any transcripts of those comments. But I wasn't surprised about that.

After Karen returned to Hobart, her new lawyer got her in front of the court for a bail hearing. She hadn't applied for bail up to this point, although she'd done nine months, three weeks and six days in prison, waiting for the charges to be formalised and heard.

The judge seemed surprised she'd been imprisoned on remand for such a long time. He asked why she hadn't made an application before this.

'The police told me not to bother, Your Honour,' Karen told the judge. 'They said I would have no hope in hell of getting bail, because they'd oppose it.'

His Honour looked stern. 'Mmm. Well, this is my court. I make those decisions, not the police. I'm retiring shortly. If you get an application before me, I'll consider it.'

So she did. And he did. And Karen continued to wait to have her case heard, on bail for over four years. Doesn't say much for the Tasmanian legal fraternity's attitude towards the five Es of legal ethics: equality, economy, expedition, evidence and equity.

◆ ◆ ◆

The case continued to inflict collateral damage. Three members of the Sue Supporters were in the public gallery of the Tasmanian Supreme Court when Karen next applied for bail. She continued her plea of not guilty to charges of perverting the course of justice and corrupting a witness. The police alleged she provided them with false information in the expectation that another person would give false evidence.

Three Sue Supporters, including Lynn Giddings, were taking notes when His Honour told a court officer that this 'should have been a closed court'.

He then said the three women could be charged with contempt of court. He told the terrified trio that they could be put straight into a lift, taken to a van and off to prison. The court officer was instructed to collect their notebooks. His Honour then tore out the offending pages and ripped them to shreds before handing the books back to the stunned women. He warned them not to contact Karen.

Section 37A of the *Justices Act 1959* (Tas) does say that an account of bail proceedings shouldn't be published – but did the judge know the three note-takers proposed to publish anything? They were there, as they always try to be, in an attempt to show those involved in this case that they aren't alone in their struggle.

◆ ◆ ◆

During this turbulent period, others were being dragged into the vortex. Eve Ash and her crew were subjected to surveillance, veiled threats and outright breaches of police procedure whenever they were in Tasmania, asking questions, filming the answers and generally stirring the pot, which police had thought was cooked enough already. It reached a point when Eve would no longer travel to Tasmania for fear she might be thrown in the clink and treated like Karen. Even her banking records and members of her crew were subpoenaed in the hope of finding she'd paid Meaghan and others for interviews, directly or indirectly, and had contributed to Karen's resolve not to roll over.

Meaghan Vass soared to public notoriety, doing more flip-flops on her sensational story than an overcooked pancake. On 4 September 2017, a police legal adviser wrote to her lawyer saying that police wished to interview Meaghan. The adviser asserted that Meaghan had made a false statement when she signed the statutory declaration saying she was on the yacht, as she had given sworn evidence at the trial that she was not, and he warned Meaghan's lawyer that, if she continued to espouse the new story, both Meaghan and her lawyer could be exposed to a charge of perverting the course of justice. A month later, Meaghan made a new statutory declaration denying that she'd been on the *Four Winds*.

In March 2019, she changed her evidence again, giving an interview on *60 Minutes* telling pretty much the story she'd included in her statutory declaration two years before. Then she again backtracked and denied that she'd been on the yacht. All her flip-flopping hasn't done her, her story or Sue Neill-Fraser any good. Meaghan's credibility has been shot to pieces. Exactly the outcome the prosecution needed.

By 2021, Sue Neill-Fraser had spent twelve years in prison. Meaghan's evidence was to be the foundation of Sue's appeal in March that year, her last roll of the dice. Meaghan was an anxious witness, but she haltingly related the same story she'd told Karen and others in 2017, telling the court the names of the two men she was allegedly with. She sat squirming in a video booth. At first she had a trusted friend beside her, but this was disallowed by the court, which ruled that only registered support people were permitted. She told the court she was five months pregnant and the lead judge, Justice Helen Wood (who coincidentally knew some of the back story to Meaghan's appearance, having presided over some of Karen's bail hearings), offered several times to allow her a break, or time to confer with her lawyer, who was present in court.

Poor Meaghan! Anyone who saw her desperation in the witness box would understand how she felt when she saw her evidence – the names and photos of the men she told the court were on the *Four Winds* with her that night – covering the front page of the Hobart *Mercury* the following day. She fell apart.

The DPP, Mr Coates SC, was in his element, determined to prevail. It wasn't his finest performance. Even the judge intervened at times to enable Meaghan to catch her breath between the barrage of questions. Some of his questions were so argumentative that they sparked intakes of shock or dismay from the Sue Supporters in the court. Their gasps were so noticeable that Justice Wood gently admonished them, saying, 'Mr Coates is doing his job.' Well, he certainly did a job on Meaghan.

When he finally accused her of 'making it all up for *60 Minutes*', which was demonstrably incorrect, she just said, 'Yes, yes! Can I go now?'

Sue, watching on via videolink along with her legal team, felt Meaghan had suffered enough. Reluctantly, after a meeting with Sue, Robert Richter QC pulled away the main plank supporting Sue's appeal. He advised the court that Sue no longer relied on any of Meaghan's evidence, allowing her to flee from the DPP's blitzkrieg. Meaghan's legal adviser was given several opportunities to visit his client during her evidence and offer support, but he didn't protect her.

Meaghan later lodged a complaint about his failure in this regard, but the Legal Profession Board exonerated him. Because of the unwritten rules protecting the Establishment in Tasmania, they don't rush to finish investigating complaints from the public about their members, who form the Establishment they protect.

The key issue here was whether Meaghan's evidence could be made subject to a suppression order to prevent it appearing in the media. But the Legal Profession Board said Meaghan's legal adviser couldn't seek suppression orders about her evidence because he 'had no standing' in that hearing. This is rubbish. Usually, a lawyer makes a submission to the judges to consider suppressing evidence and seeks a ruling. Many disagreed with the claim that Meaghan's lawyer had no standing because of his other interactions with the judges during the hearing. But even if he didn't have standing, he had every opportunity to convey Meaghan's wishes to Sue's legal team, who could have raised the issue. It was a debacle from start to finish. Poor Sue!

Anyway, Meaghan's complaint came too late. Sam was out of the bag and on the front page. Don't kid yourself that picturesque little Hobart is Tinsel Town. The criminal undercurrents run fast and hard below the surface, and Meaghan had every right to be terrified. She still is.

◆ ◆ ◆

In the years since Karen was tormented, isolated and starved, she has never been brought to trial on the charge of perverting the course of justice. The police have dangled it over her in an ongoing power play – 'Look what we can do to you if we want to.' They threw in gun-trafficking charges as well, just to confirm the criminality of her offences. Being on bail over the years until her case was heard has required a monthly court hearing, which has meant about sixty appearances, mentions or directions hearings by her court-appointed lawyer and someone from the DPP's department before a Supreme Court judge. A grand use of court resources and everyone's time, and a total disdain for those five Es of due process.

Karen has had to put up with police stopping her when they spot her out in the city and pulling her into the police station for 'a little chat' on some ridiculous pretext. Then, when that was dealt with and she asked if she could go, they'd suggest that 'Sam' (Detective Sinnitt) was just next door. 'Do you want to change your mind on the Sue stuff?'

A recent 'little chat' involved her being pulled in to view a CCTV video, allegedly of her stealing items from a Telstra shop. When Karen saw it, she laughed. 'Are you serious?' The girl in the video was about twenty, wearing a T-shirt and wheeling a toddler in a pram.

'Twenty years younger than me,' she told me later, 'I don't have a toddler and she didn't have any tatts on her arms. I fear for the safety of Hobart with those dickheads in charge.

'I got up to walk out and got offered a chat with Sam again. "He's just next door," they told me. I told them to fuck off. Cops will have to work harder than that to flip me. I've hung on for more than four years.'

She hasn't cracked.

Somebody dobbed her in about her circle of friends, one of whom is the head of a leading motorcycle club in Tasmania. He's a good protector. He may be a bikie, but he holds a Working with Children certificate and counsels adults with challenging behaviours. But the welfare considered her children were in danger and planned to remove them to foster families. Fortunately, Karen's mother stepped up and volunteered to retire early. As a 'temporary' solution, she took over the kids, then aged six and eight. She'd planned to work for a couple more years to give herself a better financial base and get all the odd jobs done around home before retiring, but she loves those kids and didn't want them to go to foster care. She's another victim of this saga.

I found it concerning that the bias against Karen had filtered down to the uniformed street cops. Why else would they keep dragging her into a police station for a 'little chat'? It's a form of harassment. The real reason emerged when Justice Wood, who has patiently sat through endless hearings going nowhere, said at a recent hearing that Karen's case had been dragging on too long, and her court was keen to see an outcome. No more wasting court's time (for which read hers). So the DPP had to put up or shut up. Subsequently, surprise, surprise, all the conspiracy charges and several gun charges were dropped, leaving Karen to face only one charge: 'possession of a firearm', relating to a gun found in a car she was driving at the time.

She was sentenced for that offence, to which she pleaded guilty on 20 July 2021. She copped six months suspended for time already served.

Jeff Thompson had to wait until November 2021 to discover his fate. The case was adjourned yet again (DPP still 'not ready') until February 2022.

Along with the others mentioned in this story, Sue's daughters and their families have lived and breathed this case for twelve years. Sarah, one of her daughters, has become an expert media performer, being the front person for all the many media inquiries about her mother's case; her husband Mark, a senior public servant, has used up all his holiday leave over the last twelve years to support Sarah at court hearings. Their children don't know their grandmother other than through prison visits, which the elder child has started to find too stressful. Although lawyers have donated hundreds of *pro bono* hours, the family's money, Sue's inheritance and her daughters' futures are gone. The ripples spread wider and wider.

During Sue's first appeal in 2012, the appeal judges found that the trial judge had said 'there was no direct evidence that the appellant killed the deceased' and 'no direct evidence of the circumstances of the homicide'. Despite this, the appeal judges said that the judge in Sue's original trial 'thought it *quite likely* that the appellant hit the deceased on the head with a *heavy wrench* from behind, but concluded that the evidence did not enable the making of a detailed finding as to the manner of attack'. [My emphasis.]

Well, a 'quite likely' scenario is not good enough. The judge's comments were not just based upon an insufficiency of evidence but upon a total absence of it, as the judge acknowledged, and they were clearly contrary to the most basic legal principles. The image of the Tasmanian legal system has taken a pounding over the years, as evidenced by a public comment posted on social media: 'Be afraid "normal" Tasmanians, be very afraid! This could happen to you too!!'

Here is Karen reflecting on her new awareness of self:

> *I've hated this woman. I've not loved her at full capacity. I've fed her lies & told her she wasn't good enough. I've let others tell her she wasn't good enough, too. I've allowed her to be broken. I've allowed others to treat her disrespectfully. I've allowed her to run through brick walls and battle for others who wouldn't even stand up for her. I couldn't stop individuals from abandoning her, yet I've seen her get up and stand to be a light to others & love others despite all that. I have stood paralysed by fear while she fought battles in her mind, heart, and soul.*
>
> *This woman has screwed up many times, as a daughter, lover, and friend, because she doesn't always say or do the 'right things'. She has a smart mouth, and she has secrets. She has scars ... because she has a history.*
>
> *Some people love this woman, some like her, and some don't care for her at all. She has done good in her life. She has done bad in her life. She is random and sometimes silly. She will not pretend to be someone she is not. She is who she is ...*

You can love her or not love her. But, if she loves you, she will do it with her whole heart. She will make no apologies for the way that she is. This woman is a WARRIOR & A SURVIVOR. She's not perfect but she has a lot of WORTH!

Further reading on the Sue Neill-Fraser case

Books

Murder by the Prosecution, Andrew Urban (Wilkinson, 2018).
Death on the Derwent, Robin Bowles (Scribe Publishing, 2018).
Southern Justice, Colin McLaren (Hachette, 2019).

Film

Shadow of Doubt – Eve Ash

Six-part TV series

Undercurrent at <https://www.imdb.com/title/tt9606838/>

Journalist blog

Wrongful Convictions, edited and written by Andrew Urban at <https://wrongfulconvictionsreport.org/> (free subscription)

Podcasts

The Man Who Wasn't There by Hugh Selby
Who Killed Bob? by Eve Ash

Sue Supporters contact

somuchdoubt@gmail.com
Rosie 0407547785

Etter–Selby papers

These can be found at <LCTP14_31_08_2021.pdf/Parliament of Tasmania

Ombudsman's report on Jeff Thompson's RTI application

<https://www.ombudsman.tas.gov.au/__data/assets/pdf_file/0009/575244/O1804-116-Decision-Final-Signed.PDF>

Chapter Five

THE VANISHING EVIDENCE

Noel Han is an Australian of Chinese heritage. In 1992, he was thirty-five years old, working in Sydney as a forklift driver, with good prospects for the future. He'd been married and had two young children, a son and a daughter, but the marriage had broken up and he was now living with a girlfriend by the name of Tracy*.

Then, in the dead of night on 12 June 1992, one of Noel's workmates, Sam Rolls, was brutally attacked in his apartment. Police alleged that Rolls was having an affair with Tracy and that Han had gone to Rolls's flat between 2 and 3 am, after the two men had finished their work shift, and inflicted severe head injuries on him, leading to his death the following afternoon. More than two years later, on 15 June 1994, Noel was convicted of murder.

Sam Rolls was a large, strong man; at 182 cm tall, he was about fifteen centimetres taller than Noel Han. Crime-scene photos of Rolls's injuries showed an incredible amount of damage. The victim had been bashed to death, but he'd put up quite a fight. The flat was trashed and Rolls's blood was found all around the debris.

Noel Han insisted he was a friend and workmate of Sam Rolls and often visited his friend at his flat. His version of events was that he'd gone to Sam's flat after work that night, and they'd spoken about the rumours that Sam was having an affair with Tracy. They were still talking when two men burst in and demanded that Noel leave. Taken by surprise, he hesitated, so one of them kicked him in the leg and the other, a tall, skinny man, hit him on the back of the head. Noel fought back; he king-hit one of them, then 'got the hell out of there', he said.

Rolls had told Noel that two weeks earlier, he'd arrived home late and seen two men breaking into a doctor's surgery next door. They spotted Rolls looking out of the window, and he told a couple of friends he'd overheard one of them say, 'He's going to rat on us.' Rolls also told a family member he was worried that these two men might come back to get him, as he'd looked out the window again to see if they were still there.

Rolls immediately called the police, but the men fled before they arrived. The burglars were still at large at the time of Rolls's death. Noel Han thinks the men were possibly after drugs; when they realised they'd been seen, they blamed Rolls for calling the police and came back that night to confront him.

The next day, Rolls's girlfriend let herself into his flat after being unable to contact him. She found Rolls semi-conscious and seriously injured – and naked apart from one sock. He was taken to hospital but died at 7.52 pm.

Police were called and inspected the flat. They concluded there'd been a fight in which Rolls was hit with a hard, blunt instrument. No apparent weapon was found in the apartment.

Noel was interviewed by the police on Monday 15 June, because they'd heard he had a grudge against Rolls for allegedly sleeping with his girlfriend. Noel admitted he'd been to the apartment on the night of 12 June. He voluntarily participated in this interview. He told the police about the two men and said that he'd been forced out of the flat, leaving his friend with the intruders. He described the men to the detectives. When they asked about the intruders' hair colour, he said that one of them had light brown hair and the other was sandy-coloured.

After this interview, police took Noel to Sam Rolls's apartment and then to Penrith police station, where they made a record of interview. Noel Han says that 'during this whole ordeal, the police insisted that

I was only assisting the police with their inquiries.' (My strong advice to everyone I meet is to *never* help police with their inquiries. Let them do their own job!) After the interview, Noel was charged with the murder of Sam Rolls. He was photographed, and samples were taken of his blood and hair.

These events set Noel Han on a path to almost sixteen years in custody. He wasn't released until 6 December 2009, having served his maximum sentence of fifteen years and seven months. Throughout his term in jail, he continued to proclaim his innocence. His minimum term expired on 5 December 2005, four years before his release, but to gain early release he would have had to confess to the murder, which he refused to do. For the Serious Offenders Review Council, confession was a prerequisite for obtaining parole.

'I refused to see them,' he told me. 'I was wrongly convicted.' He was reclassified from A2 (maximum security) to B (medium security) to serve out his time. He left prison aged fifty-two, unemployed, broke and homeless.

It's been my experience, supported by many professionals who work in the area of unsafe convictions, that most accused criminals loudly proclaim their innocence, guilty or not, until they're sentenced. From then on, the guilty usually settle in to do their time, but those who truly believe they're innocent badger every person they meet about their story.

Noel was one of those people. Day in and day out, counting off the weeks and months, Noel seethed in his cell, refusing to believe that the truth wouldn't get him out. He was an angry and embittered man, keeping to himself and surviving tough prison time as best as a 'cleanskin' can.

He saw and experienced dreadful and degrading things to which he should never have been exposed. He was an innocent man in the clutches of New South Wales Corrective Services, who were renowned for denying prisoners decent treatment. He fumed at the police, who had sat on evidence that might have exonerated him.

The prosecutor had falsely accused him and had produced bizarrely inappropriate witnesses, including a clairvoyant; his lawyer didn't ask enough questions; and the judge and jury and society in general were against him.

This is Noel's story.

◆ ◆ ◆

Police obtained various samples from Sam's unit and took photos. After Sam died in hospital, his body was transported to the morgue, and at 10 am the following day, 13 June 1992, a forensic pathologist, Dr Ellis, began an autopsy.

During the autopsy, Dr Ellis concluded that Rolls had suffered at least twenty-two blows to his head and body from a 'sharp-edged, heavy instrument'. He also found several hairs stuck in the dried blood on Rolls's hand and elbow. He described these as follows:

> *There were some small patches of dried blood on the backs of both elbows. With the dried blood on the left hand I observed five fibres of hairs which appeared to be light brown in colour, all of which were approximately four cms long and I found these both in the palm of the hand and on the back of the index finger.*
>
> *On the outer surface of the left upper arm I observed four longer fibres or hairs, each approximately 15 cms long and also fairly light in colour.'*
>
> *These were labelled and bagged for forensic examination as follows and given to Constable Ian Beatty, who was involved in the investigation.*
>
> *Item 1: Five light brown coloured hair fibres, approximately 4 cms long and*
>
> *Item 2: Four fairly light-coloured hair fibres approximately 15 cms long.*

In view of the discovery of these hairs, Constable Beatty returned to the flat on Sunday 14 June with Dr Ellis and Detective Poulteney. Beatty said:

> The prime reason was so that Dr Ellis could view the crime scene … It was then that I noticed the state of the carpet in the unit. [It] was grubby and appeared not to have been cleaned for some time. On closer inspection … I saw numerous hairs/fibres on the carpet throughout the unit. At the time I discussed the matter with Poulteney and Ellis and formed the opinion that the hairs/fibres found on the deceased's hand more than likely came from the carpet. [My emphasis.]

Beatty decided that, on the balance of probabilities, the hairs were not important, so no additional samples were collected for comparison or testing. But in a criminal case, the burden of proof is 'beyond reasonable doubt', not an assessment of the balance of probabilities by a junior police officer.

Nevertheless, on 18 June, Beatty delivered the samples obtained from the crime scene, including the unexplained hairs listed as autopsy items 1 and 2, to forensic scientist Rudolf Wegener. Mr Wegener listed all the samples delivered to him in a report he wrote on 20 November 1992. In that report he says he received twenty-two samples in total. Item 1 was blood taken from Rolls. Item 2 was blood taken from Han. The other twenty items were samples from the flat such as swabs from walls, light switches and so on, and from cars belonging to Han, Rolls and Han's girlfriend Tracy. Han's blood was the only sample that could be linked to him. Most of the tests weren't definitively positive to Rolls either, except for his bloodstained track shoes, which were found in the flat.

The final sample in Wegener's list was labelled '22. Swabs and smears.' There was no mention of the hairs from the autopsy. In fact, the list of items on the P377 New South Wales Police Specimen/Exhibit Form prepared on 18 June 1992 wasn't consistent with the list provided by Mr Wegener in November. Item 2 on the P377, for example, was 'Blood sample taken from deceased (taken at the mortuary)', Item 22 was 'Blood sample taken from defendant' and Item 23, a later sample, was 'Swabs and smears from the deceased'. There was no mention of hair samples taken from Noel Han or supplied by Sam Rolls's girlfriend.

Beatty has said he also remembers submitting some exhibits to the Institute of Forensic Medicine. Among those exhibits, Item 23 was a collection of 'swabs and smears from the deceased'. He had a discussion with the pathologist about testing hairs or fibres, but was told:

> the Division of Forensic Medicine were unable to examine the hairs/fibres as they required multiple samples, in the vicinity of 50, with root follicles attached before they could do anything with them. I was informed … that they were unable to do any tests.
> The hairs/fibres [in question] would have remained with the smears and samples [from the deceased] as they would have been sealed in the same bag.

This surprised me. I was concerned that Beatty had lumped different types of samples in one evidence bag, and it was strange that the pathologist was so reluctant to test the hairs. Trichology, the scientific study of hair, has been around since the nineteenth century, and forensic scientists use it in three major ways. Chemical assays of hair can be used to assess the use of illegal drugs, screen for the presence of heavy metals in the body or test for nutritional deficiencies. The root follicles contain DNA, which can be analysed. Finally, microscopic comparison of hairs collected from different places can be used to determine if the hairs are from the same source.

I already knew that there were established models that allow human hair to be identified as being from people of European, Asian or African ancestry. Europeans' hairs are usually straight or wavy, with round or oval cross-sections, and have fine to medium-sized pigment granules distributed evenly on the shaft of the hair. Hairs from people of Asian ancestry are straight, have circular cross-sections and have medium-sized pigment granules that are grouped in patches. The outer layer of the hair shaft, known as the cuticle, mainly consists of dead cells; this may be thicker among people of Asian descent. Hairs from people of African ancestry are usually curly or kinky, with an oval cross-section.

Microscopic analysis is used to determine the characteristics of the hair and compare hairs of unknown origin, usually from the crime scene, with hair from a suspect. Two microscopes magnify the samples up to 400 times their actual size and they are compared fibre for fibre.

Surely, I thought, at some time between the 1850s and 1992, forensic services in New South Wales had acquired the microscopes and expertise required to make this distinction at least. Although results from hair composition analysis are somewhat controversial, comparison of Noel's hair with the original items 1 and 2 taken from Sam's hand and arm could have created much greater 'reasonable doubt' that Noel was the assailant. DNA was only one factor the forensic examiner could have checked. In the absence of hair roots, other exculpatory tests could have been conducted. But they were not, based on Constable Beatty's decision.

Beatty wrote: 'With the information I had in regards to the condition of the deceased's carpet and the fact that I had *exhausted my inquiries* in relation to tests on the hairs/fibres I decided that any further enquiries relating to the hair/fibres took the investigation no further.' [My emphasis.] But people charged with murder should only be convicted if they are judged to be guilty beyond reasonable doubt. I wondered when I read his report how a junior constable from a country town would have the expertise to make such a profound decision.

◆ ◆ ◆

After being arrested, Noel was in unfamiliar territory. His expertise was in using a forklift, not in criminal law. He still had faith in the justice system back then. He couldn't conceive of a jury finding him guilty on the evidence they would hear. But sometimes the jury doesn't hear the evidence that might get you over the 'not guilty' finish line, and the lawyers and the judge have a lot to do with that selection.

Lawyer Marina Voncina, who has represented Noel in several actions over the years, is passionate about her work and the clients she represents. She runs a small but busy practice in Werombi, in the far northern suburbs of Sydney. Her practice is funded mostly on the morsels doled out by legal aid, and she works long hours for little financial reward. Her website has minimal information about her; it doesn't reflect her enthusiasm and commitment to her work.

When I phoned her, she told me, 'When Noel was first interviewed by the detective, he was unaware of any postmortem examination, or any results of this examination. He didn't know about the hair fibres or anything at all that may have been found at the scene.' But the detective did know that two different types of hair fibres had been found on Sam's hand and elbow, and that the fibres found checked out with the colour and length of the intruders' hair as Noel had described it to the police.

Marina added, 'Noel is an Australian-born Chinese and he has straight black hair. You wouldn't need a microscope to work that out.'

She told me a bit about Noel's trial as well. She explained that the hair evidence had only been discussed when the jury was out of the courtroom. She said, 'Evidence in court about these other hair fibres wasn't given to the jury. The fibres were discussed in court, but they were never presented as exhibits for the jury to examine and to look at. What the police tried to indicate was that those hair fibres were probably picked up from hair fibres on the ground on the carpet.'

In fact, the police fought quite hard to avoid producing these hairs. They not only failed to produce Items 1 and 2 as exhibits, but they couldn't support their claim that lots of fibres had been present on Rolls's floor either, as no photos were taken on the first examination or Beatty's second visit. No similar hairs were found stuck to Sam's naked body either, although there was quite a bit of blood to which they could have attached.

Marina said, 'One would expect that if there were hair fibres on the carpet, it wouldn't have been limited to the blood that was on the hands and elbows of deceased, but other parts of the deceased's body, either in his clothing or other parts of his body where there was blood.'

Noel said he felt certain that Rolls must have grabbed the hair of one or both of his assailants during the struggle after Noel had departed. He added that many people have since viewed the murder scene and autopsy photos and said that one man couldn't have been responsible for all that destruction.

A problem for Han was that Tracy, his former de facto, told the police she'd woken at 7 am on the morning of 12 June to see Han standing in their bedroom with blood on his clothes and bleeding from cuts on his head. She claimed he told her he'd visited Sam and said, 'He won't bother us again.'

Noel said Tracy had embellished the truth. He admitted he had injuries caused by Sam Rolls, but they were occasioned when Sam went for one of the intruders. As Noel described the incident, 'Sam Rolls had a look on his face like if he was expecting them, and Sam had a metal object on hand, and they struggled for possession of it.' This struggle was still going on when Noel left.

He said he was concerned he might be in trouble for having a go at Rolls, so he stripped off his bloodstained clothes, put them in a garbage bag and left the garbage bag at his mother's house; his mother then disposed of the clothes, not knowing they belonged to him. If the police searched his house on the Monday, they didn't find his clothes or any potential weapon.

He didn't go to work on Friday 12 June; he went to bed for a few hours instead. He was shaken up by the fight and couldn't relax. He couldn't raise Sam on the phone and thought he must have gone to work.

That evening, Tracy drove Noel in her car to visit some friends who lived nearby, Roslyn and Barry Dalton*. Later, when police examined Tracy's car, they found blood stains that they thought might have matched Han's on the headrest; these became samples 14 and 15 given to Mr Wegener. Noel said he might have leaned back with his injured head to rest while she drove.

The Daltons gave evidence that, Noel had admitted to them and Tracy that he and Rolls had been in a fight. Barry was concerned about Noel's abrasions and took him to see a doctor at a local medical centre.

Roslyn later gave evidence that, the following morning, she heard on the radio that Sam Rolls had died as a result of injuries sustained the day before. She connected the news story with the information Noel had shared the previous night and contacted the police.

She and Barry made a statement to police on Sunday 13 July. Barry said that Noel had received lacerations on his forehead and scalp while fighting hand over hand with a tyre lever that Sam Rolls had in the apartment. The physical struggle between Noel and Sam had continued over an hour or an hour and a half. Noel said this was the first time to his knowledge that a tyre lever had been mentioned. He knew nothing of any such object.

Police also interviewed the doctor Barry had insisted he see. Dr Ramanthan said he'd seen Noel about 9 pm on 12 June. He hadn't stitched the wounds because they'd already begun healing. The doctor considered that the healing process was fairly advanced due to the 'length of time that had elapsed', and it was too late to attempt to join the edges of the cuts together. He later said in court that he remembered a laceration to the scalp about two inches long. The forehead cut was smaller.

Noel told the doctor that he'd been attacked in the street the previous day. He and Barry had agreed on this story earlier at Barry's place. He said he told that story because he didn't want to tell the doctor about his fight with Sam Rolls, which wasn't surprising. The doctor told police that the wounds were not bleeding and were consistent with having occurred in the previous twenty-four hours. The cut on the scalp was consistent with having been hit by a sharp instrument, but it was difficult to say what had made the cut on the forehead.

On Monday 15 June, Noel Han was visited by police and asked questions. He wasn't cautioned at this stage. He initially denied having been to see Sam Rolls on 12 June and told police the last time he'd seen Rolls was as they'd both left work at midnight on 11 June. To explain his lacerations, he offered the same story about having been attacked in the street.

When I asked him about it, he said, 'I remember that lie I told. It was suggested to me by a person who went Crown witness' – his friend Barry Dalton – 'and then he denied telling me that. Stupid me followed that suggestion at that time. I am not making an excuse for my stupidity, because this is what really happened. I was very vulnerable.'

He had never been in trouble with the police and was scared they would blame him for Rolls's death. He was right. When he eventually admitted to the visit and the row, even though he told police about the two menacing men who'd appeared in the flat, he was charged with the murder and remanded in custody. From 29 October 1992 until 6 May 1994, when he was sentenced, he was held in jail.

Noel told me, 'Sam Rolls's girlfriend made a statement to the police as well. Police told her that hair was found at Sam's and asked her to supply hair samples. If these hair fibres were not important, the police wouldn't be asking.' They took samples of Noel's hair as well.

At the trial, Noel saw one of the key issues as being the non-Asian hair fibres that Dr Ellis had described during the committal. He wanted his lawyer to subpoena the police to produce the hairs, but the police treated the issue as a joke. He said, 'My legal aid defence, Greg Scragg, knew well before the trial what the police were saying about these hair fibres, because when another solicitor mentioned them, Scragg was laughing about what the police were saying.'

He said that he thinks Scragg should have subpoenaed Constable Beatty to produce them. Instead, Scragg asked Beatty in the witness box, 'Have you still got those hair fibres?' Beatty responded, 'I think so.' But they were never shown to the jury and no evidence was presented about them.

Another thing that upset Noel Han about his trial was Dr Ellis's evidence about how long before his death Sam Rolls was likely to have been injured. Dr Ellis, who had examined Rolls's wounds on 13 June 1992 during the postmortem, told the court, 'They were all of similar appearance in the sense of none showing evidence of healing. So I would be happy to accept that they were probably all inflicted at approximately the same time, given that it would obviously take a period of time to actually inflict those wounds. I think that the naked eye appearance of the wounds is such that they wouldn't show any obvious changes over a few hours. So that if it took a few hours to inflict them all ... I think longer than two or three hours [before his death] it would become more unlikely. The wounds would tend to dry out. The edges would dry out, which I saw no evidence in any of that ... I can't say exactly three hours – if it was three-and-a-half to four hours possibly, but longer than that time period becomes much less likely.'

Since Sam Rolls died the previous day around 8 pm, this put the injuries inflicted on him in Kingswood at around 5 pm that day, when he was discovered, still alive, by his girlfriend and when Noel Han was at least forty-five kilometres away in Liverpool.

Noel said, 'One would think if Sam Rolls had sustained those injuries at approximately the same time as my lacerations, then Dr Ramanathan would have been able to suture me up. At the trial I heard that when Sam was admitted to hospital, still alive at that time, the anaesthetist began suturing some of his facial wounds.'

The anaesthetist's attempt to suture the facial wounds just before Rolls died may have been a case of starting somewhere, especially the face, which is more visible and heals better. Nevertheless, there did seem to be inconsistencies in this evidence.

Noel went on, 'Also, the Crown prosecutor's reason for my blood not being found in Sam Rolls's flat is I had cleaned up my blood only from the flat. How could I distinguish my blood from Sam Rolls's blood, which was everywhere?'

Prosecution witnesses also insinuated that Noel's injuries were self-inflicted, which would have been a good trick, as there was a deep five-centimetre-long cut in the back of his head.

Noel said he sat through two agonising days of his defence barrister's questions being put to a Crown witness who was a clairvoyant, 'who gave evidence in the box about having a premonition of Sam Rolls's murder. She goes wandering through her local cemetery having out-of-body experiences, feeding biscuits to her dead cat Snowy. My barrister kept this person in the witness box for two-and-a-half days, instead of dismissing her as an unreliable witness.'

Maybe Scragg thought he'd try to make her look that way in the witness box.

Noel said Scragg visited him in Long Bay and suggested he plead contrition before he was sentenced. Noel said Scragg told him if he didn't, there would only be one way out of Long Bay – in a box. Noel lost it and told Scragg he was sacked.

Noel gave evidence at the trial on his own behalf, telling the jury the real story of what happened, but he made a tactical error. 'On legal advice, I made a dock statement,' he told me, 'which was the worst thing I could have ever done. I should've got into the witness box.' Speaking from the dock, he wasn't required to swear an oath attesting that his evidence was true; giving sworn evidence from the witness box would have carried more weight.

The jury had heard several versions of the events of 12 July from police, forensic witnesses, doctors and three of Noel's former friends. There was no physical evidence to link him to the scene, and no hairs from the dead man's hand had been produced to create reasonable doubt. There were no witnesses. The prosecution case was circumstantial.

After the jury went out for their deliberations, the foreman asked the judge for transcripts of the Crown witnesses' evidence. The Crown prosecutor opposed this, arguing that the transcripts contained the legal arguments made while the jury was absent, and it would take too long to delete them. Noel's barrister supported not supplying the transcripts to the jury for the same reason.

Noel said, 'My defence should have been arguing that the jury should have the transcripts because the jury would have read the same inconsistencies that I picked up on when I received the transcripts in jail.'

During his summing up at the end of the trial, the judge told the jury that the Crown had sought to prove its case 'by a number of pieces of circumstantial evidence, the making of admissions by the prisoner to three witnesses ... and the telling of two lies by the prisoner, which it was submitted revealed a consciousness of guilt on the part of the prisoner'.

Courts can accept evidence about how a defendant acts after an alleged crime is committed. The prosecutor can introduce testimony that tends to show that the defendant's actions prove he knew he was guilty (of doing something). This includes any lies the defendant has told to police or to others. The prosecutor has the burden of proving the defendant's intent, so anything done to throw police off the scent or disguise the perpetrator's actions in regard to his alleged crime are relevant and can be used to demonstrate his feelings of guilt.

The judge also emphasised two other lies that he said were 'inconsistent with his innocence': his telling Dr Ramanthan that the injuries to his head were the result of an assault at Liverpool, and his initially telling police that he'd last seen Sam Rolls at work on Thursday 11 June.

The judge went on, 'Before you can use the telling of a lie by the accused as conduct by the accused amounting to an implied admission by him of his guilt of the crime charge and hence as conduct by him inconsistent with his innocence strengthening the

Crown case, you must be satisfied in relation to the alleged lie of all of the following things.

'Firstly, that the accused said what the Crown alleges he said. For example, that the accused said that he'd received the injuries to his head when he was assaulted at Liverpool.

'Secondly, that what the accused said was untrue. For example, that he did not receive the injuries to his head when he was assaulted at Liverpool.

'Thirdly that what the accused said was a lie, that is, that at the time the accused said what he said he knew it was untrue and he deliberately, consciously lied.

'Fourthly, that what the accused said was on a matter which was material to his guilt or innocence of the crime charged.

'Fifthly, that the accused told the lie out of a consciousness of guilt of the crime of murdering Sam Rolls and out of a fear that if the truth emerged about the matter on which he lied, the truth would implicate him in the offence – that the accused told the lie because telling the truth would reveal the accused had some knowledge of the killing of Sam Rolls and telling the truth would implicate the accused in the killing of Sam Rolls.'

The jury didn't believe Noel's version of events, and he was found guilty of the murder.

The trial ended on 6 May 1994. On Friday 18 November 1994 – a very long time to be sitting in prison not knowing your sentence – the court finally re-convened before Justice James to hear Noel's sentence. The judge acknowledged that 'it is regrettable the holding of proceedings on sentence has been delayed so long.'

In the meantime, Noel had sacked his legal aid team and commenced an appeal against his conviction. The judge commented at the sentencing proceedings that Noel was unrepresented, although Noel told me he'd represented himself. Didn't do him much good.

During sentencing, the judge observed that 'consistent with the defence case at the trial, that the prisoner wasn't the person who had killed Sam Rolls, the prisoner had not claimed that he had acted in self-defence'. That was one potential mitigating factor out the window.

It seemed, though, that the judge may have experienced some misgivings about the evidence given by Roslyn and Barry Dalton about admissions Noel had allegedly made to them, as he'd left it open to the jury. His Honour didn't seem in any doubt about the rest of the evidence, and he was not unduly swayed by numerous references Noel had tendered about his previous good behaviour and character.

Justice James said he was satisfied that Noel had been motivated by feelings of sexual hostility towards Rolls. Though Noel may not have intended to kill him with a tyre lever (which never showed up), he was convinced Noel 'at least contemplated the possibility of physically assaulting Rolls'. The judge sentenced Noel Han to fifteen years and seven months with a minimum of eleven years and seven months, including time already served. His appeal was subsequently dismissed.

Noel was sent to Lithgow correctional centre and recorded some recollections on his sentence there.

He remembers being called to the office and informed that SORC wanted to see him.

'What's SORC?' he asked.

The officer said, 'Serious Offenders Review Council.'

Noel said, 'No, I am not seeing them at all. I am maintaining my innocence.'

The officer said, 'You will not get parole.'

Noel said, 'They can take their parole and shove it up their arse.' From that day throughout his sentence, he was never seen by SORC.

Noel's memoir continued, 'There were nine people in our family, and my sister Leonie and my mum were the only ones who visited me when they could.

'My ex-partner brought the children, Cameron and little Belinda, to see me soon after my prison term started. She said, "Have a good look at them. They will not be coming again." She told the kids I was in prison for life.

'I had to be cruel to be kind and stop my mum from visiting me, as she was getting old and spending a good eight hours on public transport. Not long after my mum stopped visiting me, there was a train derailment in the Blue Mountains and my mum said that she would have been on that train.'

Noel's kids had a tough time too. His former partner was in a relationship with someone else and was finding it difficult to manage two children. She claimed seven-year-old Cameron was uncontrollable, so she asked welfare services to come and take him away.

Belinda remembers it vividly. She told me, 'I loved my big brother so much. These big people came and dragged him out. He was hanging onto Mum's arm crying, "Please don't send me away, Mum!" I was screaming as well. I'll never forget it. They took him to a children's home in Newcastle. He had a horrible life. We both went through hell and back.'

◆ ◆ ◆

Noel Han didn't sit on his hands during his prison sentence. He refused to accept that he had to do time for a murder he didn't commit. He began a letter-writing campaign, using at least eleven reams of A4 paper and spending $367 on pre-paid stamped envelopes, in an effort to prove he hadn't killed Rolls. He wrote to parliamentarians, professors of law, lawyers, Freedom of Information, the New South Wales Attorney General's Department, police, forensic services personnel, the innocence projects that were beginning to spring up in the early 1990s, and even to the media.

In my experience, people who never deviate from claiming they're innocent long after the last legal appeal avenue has been explored quite often are just that. At any time in Australia, experts have estimated that up to four per cent of convicted prisoners are doing time for crimes they didn't commit. It may not seem all that many, but you wouldn't want to be one of them.

Evan Whitton has been reporting on corruption for more than twenty years and has won five Walkley awards. In his book *Serial Liars*, he quotes law reform campaigner A. P. Herbert as saying that 'error and injustice are built into the legal system'. This wouldn't matter so much if the system were better at rectifying its errors.

Without firm and constant pressure from the outside, the legal system is reluctant to correct its mistakes. People who have been convicted of a crime can use the appeal process – but only if they're permitted, as appeals are not automatic. And once those avenues are exhausted there's not much a convicted felon can do unless there's an external cheer group that believes in their innocence and is prepared to chip away at the barriers. If the process of conviction was flawed, the prisoner pays the price. And Noel Han thought fifteen years was a very high price indeed.

He heard about Marina Voncina and enlisted her aid. She tried several avenues with no success, including going to the media. She was very concerned about the non-production of the hairs. She accepted that the hair evidence might not exonerate Noel, but she was indignant that it hadn't been produced.

Noel Han wrote thousands of pages from his cell, trying to get access to the hairs in order to have them examined. The police closed ranks. They either didn't answer or thwarted his requests. Freedom of Information did the same, referring him back to police.

In mid-August 2000, Noel saw an article in the *Sydney Morning Herald* saying that the New South Wales police minister, Paul Whelan, had announced the establishment of a state government DNA justice panel, modelled on a similar panel at the University of Wisconsin's law school. The panel would be accountable to the police minister and would be made up of a mix of members, including representatives of the Privacy Commissioner, DPP and police.

It was proposed that, if an applicant could show the justice panel that DNA tests might overturn their conviction, the panel would have the authority to request tests be conducted on 'items that may never have been analysed or not considered during a trial'. The panel was to start operating in July 2001. The newspaper cited various cases of injustice that had been subsequently overturned (many after the accused had spent far too many years in jail).

The examples cited were Ziggy Pohl, Alexander Lindsay and Douglas Rendell, who had all been convicted of murders they didn't commit and were subsequently financially compensated. I wondered how you'd work out an appropriate sum.

Noel was buoyed up by this article and sent even more letters from his cell. He was determined to get those hairs produced, and he was convinced the man who knew where they were was Constable Beatty. After all, at Noel's trial in 1994, Beatty had said under oath that he 'knew where they were'.

New South Wales corrective services moved Noel around various prisons, including Bathurst, where he was when his mother died. He wrote to me later:

> *Whilst I was at Bathurst Correctional Centre in 2004, my mum passed away. I was called to the governor's office to fill out the forms to attend mum's funeral. The prison welfare officer didn't make any contact with me, neither did the clinic, to find out my mental health.*
>
> *They never did take me to mum's funeral. Not long after, my brother Neil passed away. The governor asked me did I want to fill out the forms to attend my brother's funeral. I said, 'What is the point living in hope? You didn't take me to my mum's funeral.' Once again welfare and the clinic didn't make any contact with me.*

Noel's sister Leonie informed the centre of both deaths through the switchboard. In 2005, when his other brother Warren passed away, Noel wasn't informed at all.

That's a lot of family deaths to deal with in one year, alone in prison.

◆ ◆ ◆

The volume of paper generated in Noel's search for the hairs was overwhelming. He sent hundreds of requests, concentrating on the justice panel, and eventually he heard that they had accepted his application. At last Marina and others who believed in him had a back-up squad. Noel was over the moon. Even though his sentence would probably expire in 2005, he was hell-bent on proving his innocence. Throughout 2003 and 2004, he generated a snowstorm of foolscap pages, all asking for the hairs to be produced.

Investigations were carried out at all levels but, unfortunately, the trail kept ending at Beatty. Although Dr Ellis had confirmed at the trial that he'd seen the hairs, removed them from Rolls's body and counted them into evidence bags, which he then handed to Beatty, things went cold after that. No mention of hairs on Beatty's list of evidence. No mention on Wegener's list of samples.

On 4 February 2003 the Innocence Panel at the University of Technology Sydney sent an application on Noel's behalf asking that a proper search be conducted for 'the two sets of fibres or hairs found in the hand and on the elbow of the victim'. The police end of this request was managed by Mr Bruce Ings from the police commissioner's secretariat, who contacted Penrith's area commander asking that those hairs be produced. The Penrith area commander wrote to the commissioner's office in May 2003 saying he'd been advised (by Beatty in a report) that '*it is feasible* those items were included with "Swabs and smears from deceased"'. [My emphasis.] Why would the area commander accept the feasibility of such an unlikely situation?

He added a final comment to his very thorough two-and-a-half-page report. He said:

> There is little doubt hair/fibre was taken from the body of the deceased and handed to Constable Beatty. That is clearly documented. The records after that do not reflect those items ... Hence, I am unable to establish what happened to those items. Given Constable Beatty's suggestion he gave evidence

about the items in question at the trial of Han, an examination of
his transcript of evidence may provide some clues as to what
happened to the items.

But no 'evidence' was given at the trial. Counsel had argued about whether or not to produce the exhibits in the absence of the jury, but they were never presented.

Seven months after the panel had taken on Noel's case, he received a letter signed by its chair, Mervyn Finlay QC, telling him that the fibres and hairs he was seeking had been destroyed in 1997.

Some time after being told of the destruction of the evidence, Noel heard on the prison grapevine that the New South Wales Innocence Project was being suspended by police minister John Watkins. The panel had agreed to seek DNA evidence at the request of a man convicted of a young woman's rape and murder. The case had been widely publicised, and the thought that the verdict might be nullified had sparked vocal opposition from the victim's family and others involved in the original trial. A new trial could mean new publicity, new evidence, questions being asked of investigating police and adverse effects on those near and dear to the victim, who'd thought the case was done and dusted and the bad guy was in jail. The DNA analysis found that the samples did not contain DNA from the convicted man, but by the time it was reported, the panel had been suspended.

The minister asked Mervyn Finlay QC, the chair of the panel, to conduct a review of its operations. The minister said that he didn't believe there were sufficient checks and balances to protect the victims of crime from further anguish. He said the process 'leaves too many questions unanswered. It should be more transparent, for applicants, victims and their families.'

Mr Finlay's review of the panel's operations affirmed that 'there was a clear need for a Panel' and suggested that a name change to DNA Reference Panel or similar might be a good idea. He argued that the panel should be empowered to order searches for evidence that might exculpate applicants and order tests; that the interests of the victims of crime and the public interest should be taken into consideration; and that, 'Persons convicted of an offence carrying a *maximum sentence of not less than twenty years* be eligible to apply to the panel.' [My emphasis; this is usually considered a life sentence in Australia.] The panel should also have discretion to accept applications in other 'special circumstances'.

Mr Finlay recommended that the *Crimes Act 1900* (NSW) be amended 'to require the long-term retention of forensic material found at the scene of a serious crime to facilitate post-conviction analysis'. This was a perceptive suggestion; when the Crimes Act was passed, the rozzers were barely getting their heads around fingerprinting. Mr Finlay also recommended that the panel have power to disclose information about the results of testing to applicants and other people, and that it should be able to refer matters to the Court of Criminal Appeal 'where it considers that new scientific evidence raises a reasonable probability that the Court would quash the conviction or order a new trial'.

But after Mr Finlay's report was completed, everything went quiet. Some panel members weren't even told about the report. There were just no more meetings, and funding was withdrawn.

Locked in his cell, Noel had no idea this process was under way, though he'd heard that the panel was suspended. But in November 2003 he did hear that the ABC's Radio National program *Background Briefing* intended to do a program on innocence projects and unfair convictions. Marina Voncina would be interviewed about Noel's efforts to find his evidence; Noel had been invited to participate, but he wasn't permitted to speak to the ABC.

One of the other guests was Rubin Carter, a famous American boxer who had spent twenty years in jail for a murder he didn't commit. He was eventually cleared after an Innocence Project rechecked the DNA on evidence from the crime scene.

Moderator Katrina Bolten told the audience that Carter had been 'within spitting distance of the world middleweight Crown' when he was sentenced to three life sentences for a brutal murder. She commented, 'It takes twenty years before a team of crusading citizens uncovers evidence to convince the courts what Rubin Carter's been claiming all along – he's innocent.'

American Rob Warden, head of the Center on Wrongful Convictions at Northwestern University in Chicago, said that the number of exonerations achieved in the USA had proved to be 'amazing'. As of November 2003, when the program went to air, more than a hundred people had been released from Death Row. He added, 'In Illinois, almost 6 per cent of all people who have been sentenced to death under the current law have later been shown to have been innocent.'

Background Briefing also interviewed Lynne Weathered from the emerging Griffith University innocence project. I had spoken by phone to Lynne on several occasions and knew how keen she was to get her project functioning. She said, 'We're not naïve enough to think that everyone writing to us is going to be actually innocent of the crime and we're not saying that there are large numbers of people in our prisons that are innocent. We think the system gets it right pretty much most of the time. But we have our own cases, known cases, of wrongful conviction here. So I guess what I am essentially saying is we can't just ignore everybody's claim of innocence because we think that some of those claims are false.'

Marina Voncina managed to get in a plug for Noel's case. She explained how the hairs found on Sam's body couldn't have been Noel's, but were never shown to the jury. She emphasised the devastation Noel felt on receiving the letter telling him the hairs had disappeared.

Marina said, 'If Noel knew that he had to continue to serve his sentence and even at the end of the sentence was found to be innocent, I think he could live, you know, accept that to a large degree, because at least his innocence would be proved ... He can't even do that now, no matter how much time he serves in prison.'

Moderator Katrina Bolton ended by saying, 'Noel Han won't be released from prison until 2009. And he isn't the only prisoner to discover evidence is gone forever. Even today, everywhere except New South Wales, where there's a moratorium, crime-scene evidence is still being destroyed.'

Noel felt he'd done pretty well out of the profile-raising of the little campaign he was waging from jail. However, not long after this he received the toughest blow of all, in the form of a letter from the UTS Innocence Project, dated 18 May 2004, to say that they wouldn't be able to help him because their operations had been suspended. The letter closed by saying, 'We know this letter will come as a disappointment.'

That was the understatement of the year for Noel Han. There was now no hope of proving his innocence.

On 5 December 2005, he became eligible for parole, but he wasn't allowed to leave prison early, despite being a model prisoner and completing the judge's minimum term, because he insisted on his innocence. In 2007, eighteen months into the parole period, the State Parole Authority again refused parole because Noel maintained his innocence and didn't take part in their programs to address offending behaviour.

Noel remarked bitterly, 'They send paedophiles out early with ankle bracelets, but not me.'

◆ ◆ ◆

Then Noel was moved to Junee, which made it hard for his sister to visit him. Towards the end of his sentence, he said, 'Some dropkick inmate tried to stab me in the eye. I was millimetres away from being blind. It was over jail politics, nothing to do with me. I lost a lot of respect from inmates for not retaliating, but as my sister said, 'You are so close to getting out, don't add time to your sentence.'

Noel's maximum sentence finally expired in December 2009, and he walked out of prison. He was a free man but had nowhere to go. No job. Few dollars. His nephew Brendan was waiting to drive him to his sister's home in Sydney.

Everything looked unfamiliar, Noel told me later. 'The modern motor vehicles looked like toy cars and the money looked like Monopoly play money. I had to go to St George Bank to reactivate my St George account. I had to produce ID for St George, so I showed them my release papers from prison.'

He had two weeks to find a job before his small Centrelink allowance would be withdrawn. His biggest problem was trying to explain where he'd been for sixteen years. People told him to lie, make up some story. He settled on a sick aunt he'd been caring for, who had now died.

He was lucky that he had a sister he could stay with, but her kids didn't know where he'd been since before they were born, so there were more lies. He wasn't offered any assistance to get back into society. Noel wrote to me, 'When I did get released I was in no frame of mind to look for work within the two weeks. Centrelink did give me an exemption from looking for work until June this year. I think I will feel better when I can drive again.'

He applied for several jobs, but it was no good. He wrote to me, 'If I was able to renew my driver's licence whilst I was inside, I could have been employed three times over, but because my licence expired, I have to sit the test again. Two questions away from the end and I failed the knowledge test. And then even if I get it, I either eat or pay for my licence. On top of having no job, I can't stay here at my sister's for too much longer and also I am being treated for depression. I have two options – going back inside or walking out in front of an oncoming truck – because life is shit at the moment.'

Worried about him, I made a few calls to Sydney to drum up some support. I called a group that helped recently released prisoners and asked them to contact Noel. He seemed brighter in his next email.

'I found a room in a boarding house in Manly $160.00 per week or $320.00 per fortnight. The Centrelink payment at the moment is $431.55 which leaves $111.55 a fortnight left over until I get rent assistance.' He joked about the kilograms dropping off him – 'I'm on the Centrelink diet.'

Later he wrote with better news. 'I got my first break from someone who knew Leonie who needed a storeman/forklift driver ASAP. On their application form it didn't ask about criminal history and I didn't volunteer any information.

'I had one day to learn everything at this new job on a Friday because the main storeman was going on holidays for four weeks come Monday morning. I was thrown into the deep end. But I got through it and at the end of my three months I was asked to work another three months. By this time, I got my driver's licence back on a full licence, which was handy as I had to drive the forklift on the road to transfer stock to another place.'

The jobs kept coming. He worked at a place that sold windows and doors but left that job – 'I was getting sick of pulling glass out of my hands every night.' Then he found a full-time position at a place selling fabric. And at last he heard from the Department of Housing, who called him in to inspect a one-bedroom unit.

He wrote, 'Signing the lease, the client officer said, "You didn't tell us that you had a job." I said, "I am telling you now." So they calculated my rent at 26 per cent of my gross earning. If I had informed the Department of Housing that I had a full-time job, I would have been taken off the waiting list.'

The bureaucracy is mind-bending!

Noel still had boxes and boxes of papers detailing his efforts to seek exoneration. He sometimes wrote about what he lost when he was caught up in the legal system. 'Before I was charged in 1992, I had a life. When someone gets caught up in the system, that's what they take, and when you have done the time served, you don't get back what was taken away from you.

'Nothing will change the fact of the time I have done. I still have dreams about that place. The only way I can explain what it was like is if you can imagine someone locking you in your bathroom for sixteen years and only letting you out when they want, at their will. I can't get used to not being inside the walls and seeing the stars at night.'

◆ ◆ ◆

If ever there was a case that could have been resolved one way or the other, it was Noel Han's. The laxity in the chain of evidence and the statutes that allowed evidence to be destroyed once someone was serving time meant that his claims couldn't be tested. If it wasn't his hair stuck in the blood on Sam Rolls's hand, would he have been exonerated? It's impossible to say, but the proposition was never tested. And Noel isn't the only prisoner to discover that evidence is gone forever. Every day, crime-scene evidence is being destroyed all around the world.

After serving his full term, Noel Han was sent out with no prior preparation, no driver's licence, no counselling, no money and no job, expected to sink or swim. He had served his full term and paid his debt in full. At the very least, assistance should have been given to make sure he wouldn't return to prison. And if he's innocent, as he claims, his treatment is a travesty of justice.

As he once said, 'I lost everything the day I was charged.'

◆ ◆ ◆

By the time Noel got a job, he'd lost more than ten kilos and was barely surviving on the 'Centrelink diet'. He still sends me progress reports from time to time. He's doing as well as he can.

He has re-established links with his two kids, who were collateral damage from his conviction. He says, 'Cameron and Belinda didn't have a childhood.' They'd been very close until Cameron was made a ward of the state, but they're close again now.

He's had a lot of health issues since his release. He's been told he doesn't have much time left. A letter from his doctor said, 'his lifespan is sadly unlikely to be long from here'. He says if he dies alone in his unit, no-one is likely to know until they smell something funny.

He wrote to me, 'Since being released, it's been difficult to adjust, as there wasn't any reintegration back into society. Certain things would trigger me off. Having dreams of being incarcerated, going through a retrial, moving jail cells and centres, being held in custody after my full term.' He suffers from PTSD, which his medical practitioners attribute to the trauma of serving a sixteen-year prison sentence for a crime he says he didn't commit. It's no wonder, in my opinion.

Further reading

For more information about hair analysis see 'Hair Analysis' in K. Lee Lerner and Brenda Wilmoth Lerner (eds), *World of Forensic Science* (Gale Cengage, 2006). Thanks to the authors for the use of their material.

For detailed information on miscarriages of justice go to Networked Knowledge at <http://www.netk.net.au/> which details at least thirty-two people who have been wrongfully imprisoned in Australia.

The full transcript of the ABC National *Background Briefing* program is at <http://www.abc.net.au/rn/talks/bbing/stories/s987727.htm>

For the review by Mervyn Finlay QC see <www.justice.nsw.gov.au/ DNA review panel>

See also *Death on the Derwent* by Robin Bowles (Scribe Publishing, 2018).

Chapter Six

IN FEAR OF HIS LIFE

It was one of those balmy nights in Far North Queensland, affectionately known as FNQ, where Victorians flock from the south during the cold winter months. FNQ in 'winter' is one of the best places to be in the world, with day after day of clear blue skies and mild temperatures. The invaders from down south swim, snorkel and sunbake while the locals go around wearing windcheaters.

It was Saturday 30 September 2018 and the rugby-mad residents of Alva Beach, about seventeen kilometres from Ayr, had prepared an outdoor TV and sound venue on a vacant lot next door to the surf club. They were going to hold a party to watch the NRL grand final between the Sydney Roosters in their maroon shirts and the Melbourne Storm in their white and purple. The game would be the season highlight, and the beer had flowed freely all day.

Tom Davy was a big, handsome aircraft engineer who had moved to Cairns from Newcastle in New South Wales, having won a contract to service local aircraft. The previous day, he'd driven the four hours from his place in Cairns to spend the weekend with his long-distance girlfriend, Candice Locke, a glamorous-looking girl who lived in Ayr and worked with animals. They'd met up on a dating app about four months earlier.

Tom's mother, Heather, has described him as a kite surfer and spearfisherman who had spent his life 'in, on and under the water'. Part of his reason for moving to FNQ was to indulge his love of outdoor pursuits. At Alva Beach that day, he and Candice had gone to check some crab pots they'd laid the day before, fished from the main beach and sunk a few tinnies.

About 6 pm, they started chatting to a couple of locals who were driving along the beach in a sand buggy. The buggy belonged to cane farmer Louie Bengoa, who was going for a spin with his mate Corey Christensen, a 37-year-old father of three. As they chatted on the beach, the four of them bonded over their shared passion for rugby, and Candice and Tom scored an invitation to watch the NRL grand final that evening on the vacant lot.

It had already been a busy day for the small contingent of police stationed at Ayr. Alva Beach hadn't seen so much action for ages. The Ayr police were tracking a fugitive who was wanted on a warrant for failing to appear in court. He'd allegedly broken into a house in Sarina, 330 kilometres south, stolen a car and driven off from a service station without paying for fuel. He drove north to Ayr, where he allegedly broke into several houses and stole another car. He intended to keep going on the highway but took the dead-end Alva Beach turn-off by mistake.

Police who were looking for him on the highway received word from Alva Beach that he had gone there, turned around and headed back. He was back on the highway heading for Cairns when the cops pulled him up. When he couldn't go any further, he rammed their police car. Not surprisingly, he ended up in the Ayr lock-up, where he was watched over by Detective Sergeant Gavin Neal, Constable Noel Dwyer and a probationary female constable.

◆ ◆ ◆

Meanwhile, Tom Davy, Candice Locke and their new-found mates joined the NRL party just as the game was starting. The crowd watched the Roosters thrash the Storm by 21 to 6, to general disappointment. Witnesses at the subsequent inquest said that Candice grew increasingly drunk as the game went on. She flirted with other guests, became loud and obnoxious and swore several times at Tom.

At half-time, Tom announced that he wanted to leave, and he became annoyed with Candice when she said she wanted to stay. They'd both been drinking, but he was still quite sober (when his blood alcohol count was taken later that night, it was only a tiny bit over 0.05) and he was embarrassed by her behaviour.

Corey Christensen's wife Jaye was watching what was going on. She later told police, 'I don't remember a lot about Tom. He was very quiet, but Candice ... you knew she was there from the get-go. She was drunk ... starting to lean, get very touchy-feely.' Jaye said that when Tom suggested they leave, Candice replied, 'Fuck you, fuck off. I'm not going.'

Jaye said she'd had a premonition that something bad would happen that night. 'As the night wore on ... I've always described it as hairs standing up on the back of my neck, the feeling that I was getting from her,' Jaye said.

Candice seemed determined to kick on with her new friends. Bengoa told Tom, 'Mate, she wants to stay. We'll look after her.'

At 9.30 pm, Candice received a text message from Tom that read:

> I've told you like six times and your either too drunk to realise what im actually saying to you or youre just stubborn as fuck and trying to cause a seen! You language is discussing in front of all these pepe you don't even know. Anyways good luck with getting home. Anyways thanks for the good time. I guess all good things come to an end.

Tom left the party at 9.39 pm and parked some distance away. As he left, he said to Candice, 'You can get home by yourself.'

Another guest at the party was Ann Phelan, who lived nearby. After Tom left, Ann saw Candice huddled in the gutter crying, obviously drunk. She asked the young woman if she needed help and told her she could sleep at her place that night if she was stranded, but Candice refused. Louie Bengoa walked over to them both and said, 'She'll be right, Ann. I'll look after her.'

Patricia Hughes, who was also there, was concerned about Louie's behaviour towards the inebriated young woman. He was also drunk, and she thought he was trying to get close to Candice after Tom had left.

Jaye Christensen was particularly worried that Louie would start driving the beach buggy while he was drunk. She demanded that he hand over the keys, but he refused. She then said that if she heard the beach buggy start up, she'd lock both Corey and Louie out of the house.

Soon after that, Jaye and Corey went home to put their children to bed. After that, Corey was ready to party on, leaving Jaye at home with their boys. Jaye said later that her greatest regret was that she didn't persuade him to stay home.

By all accounts, Corey was a man's man. He liked a drink and could be a bit domineering, especially if he'd had a few.

About twenty minutes later, Tom returned briefly to the party, spoke to Louie and again offered to take Candice home. When she refused, he drove off and parked a short distance away.

At 10.07 pm he sent another text that read:

> I'm waiting down the road for twenty minutes. Pull yourself together. Cone [sic] get a lift with me or I'll just camp here the night and you can come get your keys from me.

He sent another message four minutes later explaining that he was under some coconut palms she was familiar with and was going to sleep there for the night.

Instead of messaging him back, Candice got into Bengoa's buggy and asked to go for a ride. There were competing explanations of her request. Louie said she just wanted to go for a spin; she initially claimed that she said she wanted to look for Tom, but she was less certain about it later. In any event, Louie took off along the beach in the buggy with a carton of beer and an unknown number of Bundy and Cokes under his belt. They were gone when Corey returned to the party about 10.30 pm.

At the inquest later on, Candice Locke said she didn't remember reading Tom's message advising her of his location. She also didn't dispute the words of the many witnesses who said she was drunk that night. She said she had a drinking problem at the time.

While they were driving around in the beach buggy, Candice had a fall. She originally claimed she was shoved off the buggy, but Bengoa gave contrary evidence in court. He said Locke fell when she was 'skylarking, standing up with her arms outstretched, imitating the famous scene in the movie *Titanic*'. Whether she was shoved or not, she landed on hard, compacted sand and hurt her shoulder.

The injury turned out to be a very nasty comminuted fracture of her humerus, which can be extremely painful. Those kind of fractures are usually easy to pick, as bones bleed profusely, causing swelling and severe bruising. Anyone who looked at her should have been in no doubt that she needed medical treatment.

She said later that Bengoa, who had been 'warm and friendly' at the party, laughed at her and didn't believe she was injured. 'You'll be right, mate,' he told her. She got back on the buggy, but not for long, as she was in pain. She wanted to call an ambulance, but he just kept driving. Candice said later she felt very uncomfortable with him and desperately wanted to seek medical help. She jumped off the buggy, ran across a nearby carpark and hid behind a car.

Bengoa went back to the party. He later said that he arrived with Candice and gave her some more rum, but neither claim was correct. Candice didn't go back to the party at all.

Bengoa said the party was smaller, but Corey had returned. There would have been about ten people there, he guessed.

Two women who'd been enjoying the party from an upstairs balcony later told the inquest they saw Bengoa return alone and called out to him, 'Where's the girl?'

He didn't answer but went up to Corey and had a conversation with him. Bengoa later said, 'Corey seemed to know where she had gone.' But how could he? Corey had been at home having dinner and hadn't seen Candice. A bit later, the two men went in search of her and found her in the carpark.

When she saw that Corey was with Bengoa, Candice got back on the buggy, hoping they would go for help, but they both made light of her injuries. 'Don't be such a princess,' Bengoa told her as he drove around, very drunk. Candice was still in pain and grew upset that no-one was taking her seriously.

At around 11.30 pm, she jumped off the buggy and fled along a dirt track leading from the beach into the town, followed at a distance by the two men in the buggy. She sought refuge at the first house she saw, a holiday house at 2 Topton Street belonging to the Webber family.

◆ ◆ ◆

Inside 2 Topton Street was nineteen-year-old Dean Webber, a slightly built apprentice fitter. He'd had dinner with friends and they'd all watched the NRL final on TV, then he came home about 10.30 pm and went to sleep on the couch. He was woken about two hours later by someone banging on the door.

Webber cracked open the door and saw a dishevelled girl with a huge bruise on her shoulder, crying in pain or fear or both. 'Please help me,' she begged. 'Let me in! I'm hurt!' She explained that she'd fallen off a beach buggy, but the blokes she was with had refused to call an ambulance. She asked him to call for help.

Dean could see she was in a bad way. He let her in and locked the big glass sliding door behind her. He laid her on the couch and put ice on her shoulder. He then tried to call a couple of his friends for advice, but no-one answered; they were probably still celebrating the football game. Through the big glass door he could see a beach buggy. What he thought were two men had got down from the buggy and were standing outside. His version of how many varies in his later statements.

Dean turned the lights off, moved Locke to the kitchen and sat her on the kitchen floor in a corner, out of sight from the kitchen windows, which had no curtains. She crouched there, whimpering in pain. She'd only met these guys that afternoon, and she was terrified about what they might do to her.

Webber also sat down on the kitchen floor. He was relatively calm when he made the first call to Triple-0 at 12.26 am. In a recording of the call played later at the inquest, he told the woman on the other end about Locke seeking his help. He said, 'No, I don't know her. But she's injured.'

He broke off to yell out, 'Mate, can you go? Get off me property, mate.' Locke could be heard crying in the background.

'Please come quickly,' Dean pleaded to the operator. 'We are not safe.'

After a little while, the men gave up and went away. Bengoa later told police that they'd gone to collect Tom Davy. He wasn't hard to find, asleep in his double camper troop carrier, exactly where he said he'd be.

What did the others tell him when he woke up? Did they want him to take Candice to hospital so that Bengoa, who shouldn't have been behind the wheel of that buggy, could stay out of sight? Did they say she might be at risk from an unknown man who'd locked them both in his house?

All three men returned to Topton Street. Bengoa said he parked a short distance away and they all arrived on foot. But Dean – still on the line to Triple-0 – reported that the buggy was back. Soon after that, the operator ended the call, telling him to keep the doors locked and leave the lights out. She said she'd get someone there pronto, but he should call again if circumstances changed.

Tom Davy stood outside the door, peering in. Although all the lights were off, he was calling. 'I can see you, Candice. Come out and we'll go home.'

Perhaps both sides believed they were saving Candice that night. Dean Webber only had Candice's word to go on that she was frightened of the men in the buggy. For their part, Tom and his new friends Corey and Louie had realised she was injured and feared for the outcome. Possibly they were afraid of what it might mean for them.

Things escalated, as they often do when people have been drinking. Corey was a man who didn't like to be thwarted. Bengoa was seriously drunk. Tom was unhappy about the way the day had turned out. Perhaps Bengoa and Christensen were compounding Tom's fears that Candice was locked inside, drunk with an unknown man. The testosterone must have been raging.

The police at Ayr, however, treated the call as a 'Code 3' or routine job, eliminating any chance of a quick response. This was partly because of the fallout from apprehending the fugitive earlier in the day. Detective Sergeant Gavin Neal had been at work since 10 am, but the rest of the day's police contingent had gone home, apart from Dwyer and his female offsider, who was too junior to work alone.

Neal had arranged for a JP to sign his 'objections to bail' and other paperwork for the prisoner in the lock-up and was about to leave just after 12.30 am when the call came in from the Triple-0 operator: 'Injured woman – QAS (Queensland Ambulance Service) dispatched – disturbance outside 2 Topton Street at Alva.' It didn't seem all that urgent, and they'd need to get an off-duty officer in to cover it.

'Will I call someone in?' Dwyer asked.

Anxious to get his paperwork dealt with so he could process the man in the lock-up and go home, Neal said to Dwyer, 'How about you keep an eye on our offender and I take our young constable with me to see the JP? His house is on the way to the Alva address, and we'll look in there afterwards.' So off they went.

Ironically, the paramedics *did* treat the notification as urgent. Two female paramedics were on duty in Ayr; they arrived at Alva in minutes and pulled up 500 metres from the house at 12.33 am. They parked and waited for the police to arrive with their lights and sirens, as they'd been informed the situation could be dangerous.

At 12.42 am, on his own initiative, Constable Dwyer phoned Dean Webber. He explained that he was held up at the station because there was a prisoner in the lock-up and the other two officers were tied up with the necessary paperwork. He said they should get there within thirty minutes and told Dean to call Triple-0 if anything changed.

This was cold comfort to Dean, who was in the dark, locked inside his house with an injured girl, starting to fear for his life, with two large angry men, Davy and Christensen, yelling threats and obscenities outside. Bengoa said he'd wandered off to have a cigarette and relieve himself a short distance away.

The door to the beach house was a large glass sliding door in an aluminium frame. If it was unlocked, it could be lifted off its track without much difficulty. And, as a forensic locksmith later said in evidence, even with the locking mechanism engaged, a strong person could lift the door out of the channel by wriggling or forcing it. It's also possible that, in his haste to lock the door again after letting Candice in, Dean Webber didn't fully turn the mechanism to clip the door shut. In any event, two men had appeared outside and started rattling the door, trying to get in.

At 12.39 am, Webber sent a text message to a good friend: 'I'm about to die holy fuck I don't know what to do.'

Dean rang Triple-0 again at 12.52 pm. This time he asked for police. He told the operator, Senior Constable Luke Weiks, that two men were breaking in. '*I need police now!*'

Weiks treated the call as a hoax. He didn't grasp the seriousness of the situation. Police were always getting calls from the beachside hamlet complaining of 4WDs and beach buggies behaving in unsociable ways, so calls from Alva weren't taken too seriously.

The coroner later spent some time criticising the attitude of Weiks, who didn't believe what Dean was telling him.

Dean then put Candice on. She tried to explain the circumstances, pleading for help, but Weiks told her to stop lying. She said frantically, 'I got in the buggy; one of them – they ended up getting real crazy and pushed me out. This brings me to being right here now with this guy. They're really psycho and I don't know what to do. Are you able to help us? Is there any way?'

Weiks said, 'You've already spoken so much shit to me, though, and you do sound like you do know them.'

'This isn't a joke!' Webber shouted at the phone. 'I need police *now*!'

Weiks told him to lock himself in, but Webber said frantically, 'I can't lock myself in. They're pulling the door off.'

Yelling could be heard in the background, followed by a scream.

It's possible that the noise in the background convinced Weiks to act, or it may have been Candice's scream, but either way he said he'd send a police car. 'I'm putting a job on and sending them up to Ayr. Thank you. Bye.'

He hung up just after 12.56 am, leaving Webber to face the potential invasion alone.

◆ ◆ ◆

At Ayr police station, the incident was upgraded to 'Code 2', which meant that off-duty officers were pulled in to attend. It was pretty much a case of too little too late. When the coroner reviewed the situation, she was scathing in her assessment of the police response in general, and speculated whether Queensland police responded appropriately at all.

When the police approached the house, they were surprised to find the ambulance still sitting nearby, waiting for them. Later, when the Ethical Standards Command investigated the police response, two senior police expressed irritation that 'the ambos need them to hold their hands' at potentially dangerous incidents. But it's reasonable; police are trained to deal with threats of violence, not ambulance officers, who are trained not to put themselves in harm's way.

A lot had happened since the police were called out. At 12.57 am, barely a minute after Senior Constable Weiks hung up on him, Dean Webber made a third call to Triple-0. Clutching his phone like a lifeline, he panted out to the operator, 'I need police right now!' He said he'd stabbed 'a bloke who broke into my house … I think I've killed him.'

He said there were 'three assailants, big blokes, males', and he was 'scared … the other guy's going to kill me. I don't want to die.'

'Can you lock yourself in a room? Stay calm.'

'I don't know if I *can* stay calm.'

'Take some deep breaths. What is the name of the injured person? Do you need an ambulance as well?' The operator had a brief conversation with Candice, who confirmed the situation. She also said she'd been injured by the men on the buggy and that she was in pain and frightened.

Dean panted, 'I don't know them. They're coming back now … I've got an injured lady here … they assaulted her … three males broke in … can you please ring my mum?'

'Do you know the injured woman? Is she a friend? Does she live with you?'

'No, no, just a random person … She came here in distress.'

'What has happened to the male you stabbed?'

'He's in the street. He can't move. I think I stabbed him in the heart.' Tom had grabbed Dean's right arm, but he had the knife in his left hand. He said, 'I tried anything I could to protect myself because … he was gonna kill me … I don't know how I'm still alive, to be honest.'

Dean said he thought his leg was broken. He also said the man lying outside in the street wasn't moving. 'He could be very dead … he's lying down straight outside my house … I think I've killed him … One is coming back now … I've rung three times … he's coming back … it's not funny, not a joke … they ripped the door over the latches, three came in and pummelled me … I've never been so scared, I thought they were going to kill me … This isn't right … These people are not after valuables, they're after *us*!'

He said he'd already rung twice. 'Police said if anything changes, ring back.'

'We will send police,' the operator told him. 'They're not on duty, but we're getting them.'

The police explained to me later that in a regional outpost like Ayr, which is eighty-eight kilometres from Townsville, it wasn't just a matter of calling in a couple of off-duty members in the middle of the night, especially that weekend. It was a long weekend, and there was a big footy game on. Members could have been in Townsville, had a few drinks, gone away for a few days. But police did get a response team together, and they headed straight for Alva Beach.

'The ambulance should be on the way now. I'm going to hang up,' the Triple-0 operator said.

'No!' Dean said. 'Please don't hang up! Please stay with me ... this is not a joke ... it's not funny anymore ... this girl is in pain, she's very distressed.'

'We have everything on the way as soon as possible.'

'Please stay on the line,' Dean begged. 'When I have a police person talking to me, I'll feel safe.'

The operator agreed. She could hear Dean and and Candice comforting each other during the wait. Dean was telling Candice he'd done his best to protect her. She was comforting him. Both were in tears.

When the operator knew the police had arrived outside, she said, 'Dean, turn on the lights now.'

When he did, he cried out, 'Turn on the lights? Oh my god!! There's blood everywhere! This wasn't a good idea!'

'Don't look at the mess,' she admonished, but Webber was transfixed. 'Oh, god, there's blood everywhere,' he said. 'I'm scared ... Am I going to jail for this? I'm so scared...I tried anything I could to protect myself. There's blood everywhere. Oh my god! All I taste is blood ... I think it's all over me. I was just protecting Candice and her life.'

Because the operator stayed on the line, there's a full recording of events until after the police arrived. We hear Dean say to Candice, 'If you don't see me again, I'm sorry, I just tried to help.'

'I know, Dean, you protected me, you didn't do anything wrong ...'

It turned out that wasn't quite correct, but the fact the Triple-0 operator stayed on the line while the recording rolled on provided a great deal of clarity to later inquiries into the events at the Webbers' home that night.

At one point in the recording, the operator could be heard telling a colleague, 'I'm really worried about this young fella.' Her words couldn't have boosted Dean's confidence much. But the recorded call – and the recordings played later to the inquest – would corroborate his argument that the men were engaged in a home invasion and that Dean feared for his life and that of the woman he was protecting.

About fifty minutes after the first call to Triple-0, the police and ambulance arrived at the house together. Suddenly, it seemed as if people were everywhere, with two-way radios crackling, phones ringing, blue-and-white cars parked every which way, and revolving lights playing across the stringy scrub lining the dark track to the beach. A scene of carnage greeted them, outside and inside the house.

Tom Davy and Corey Christensen were both outside, mortally wounded. Tom had been stabbed several times, including twice in the chest, but had staggered as far as the street and made his own Triple-0 call before collapsing and dying. Corey lay in the driveway in a pool of blood, with Bengoa sitting on the ground beside him, holding his hand. Despite the paramedics' best efforts, Corey died soon after.

When the police arrived, Dean Webber ran towards the door. The operator yelled at him, 'Dean, stay away from the door! Don't go near the door. Just do as the police tell you.'

From outside the door, police were yelling, 'Get back! Get away from the door! Stand back! On the floor! Down on the floor!'

'I'm lying down now,' Dean told the operator, spreadeagled on his face in front of the couch. 'I'm handcuffed.'

His lifeline of the previous twenty or so minutes said quietly, 'I'm hanging up now.'

Senior Constable Justin Luke, one of the police who had responded to the call in the middle of the night, had gained entry through an unlocked glass door opening directly onto the lounge area, which it seemed had been the location of most of the life-and-death fighting, going by all the blood.

A trembling Dean Webber was lying face down on the floor, arms out, as he'd been instructed. He was handcuffed and cautioned. After police had checked that he wasn't seriously injured, he was told he was under arrest for murder. The waiting police took him outside to a police vehicle.

Justin Luke moved the short distance to the kitchen to check on Candice. 'Are you all right, miss?' he asked. Her reply was not very friendly. She said she was in a lot of pain.

'Is there anyone else in the house?' he asked.

'I don't think so.'

'The ambulance officers will be with you soon,' he told her. 'They're looking after someone who needs them more just now ...'

Candice didn't sound impressed. After her terrible ordeal, she just wanted to be looked after.

There were harrowing scenes outside the house that night. While ambulance crews were fighting to save Corey Christensen's life, neighbours were gathering on the periphery of the scene, confusing police about how many people were actually involved in the incident. There were people everywhere, wondering what could have happened in such a quiet street with such a quiet young man.

One of those looking on was Will Quick, Dean's best mate, who lived a few doors away. Dean had been at Will's place for dinner and the NRL match earlier that evening. Dean spent a lot of time with Will's family; his mother, Vicki, considered herself Dean's second mum, as his parents didn't live in Alva Beach

She told me later, 'Will and Dean are very close, and they'll help each other through this.' She said Will was there when the police arrived, and he saw everything.

Vicki also said that in those desperate moments when Dean feared for his life, he'd tried to phone Will, but he didn't get through. 'My son had his phone on silent that night and didn't hear it ring as Dean was calling for help, so Will suffers a lot for not helping his best mate.' The collateral damage just keeps widening in situations like this.

◆ ◆ ◆

Louie Bengoa, the last of the intruders still alive, was interviewed outside the house. The transcript shows he was incoherent, maybe from shock or maybe from the twelve beers and 'I never count the number' of rums he'd consumed that night.

He kept asking how he'd be able to face Corey's wife and children. 'He's me best mate,' he told police.

He said that Tom and Candice were an item, but they'd disagreed at the party. Tom wanted to leave but Candice wanted to stay. 'I gave her a few rums, and then all of a sudden she's like gone bang – gone a little bit funny.'

He said that later, after Candice left the buggy, he and Corey went to look for her. They got to the house at Topton Street, then went back to enlist Tom. This ties in with Dean's later evidence that one or two men came first, then 'three big men' returned.

Once they came back, they knocked and tried to get in. Bengoa said he was standing about fifteen metres away and didn't go inside the house (although Dean and Candice both said there were three of them).

Bengoa said the others hadn't been inside for long when Tom ran out saying, 'Ring an ambulance.' Bengoa was incredulous. 'I was like "What for?"' It was only then that he realised both Tom and Corey had been stabbed.

Bengoa couldn't ring Triple-0, because his phone was being recharged on a portable charger in the buggy.

But where *was* the buggy? Dean had seen it pull up, leave and pull up again, first with two men and then with three, and the sight had seriously frightened him. But by the time emergency services arrived, the buggy was nowhere in sight. When Bengoa was asked about it, he gestured vaguely down the road.

He was obviously keen to avoid drawing police attention to his driving record or his buggy. During his interview that night, the police accessed his licence details through Q-lite, a Queensland police program that allows coppers on the beat to use iPads to extract information on people and vehicles of interest.

Bengoa said, 'Oh, lucky! Are you stitching me up here?'

Did that question indicate a guilty conscience? Drink driving causing grievous bodily harm comes to mind, never mind home invasion!

Detective Paehua, who had interviewed Bengoa, reported to his superior, Justin Luke, that 'the bloke on the ground on the right is like friends with benefits with this chick on the stretcher'. All of them had been drinking on the beach or on a vacant block down the road, he said.

The police seem to have decided there was no point continuing the interview with Bengoa in his present state, so they arranged to speak to him the next day.

Louie Bengoa came to the Ayr police station on Sunday to be interviewed by Detective Senior Constable Tony Hogan. His story was more coherent than it had been the previous night, but it had changed significantly. It was also inconsistent with other participants' recollections.

In the lead-up to the party, Louie said, he left home about midday and drove a car to Corey's place. After having quite a few drinks, they decided to take the camo-coloured beach buggy for a spin, then come back to Corey's for more drinks and football.

Before the big game started, they went for another drive along the beach, where they met Tom Davy and Candice Locke (whom Bengoa referred to as 'Jacinta'). Corey's dog jumped out of the buggy near where the couple were fishing, which provided an opportunity to start a chat. The men hadn't previously met the young couple but invited them to the NRL party.

Bengoa said he provided 'Jacinta' with several rum and Cokes during the NRL game. Later, there was some tension when Tom said he wanted to leave. 'They did not really have a fight, but they had a disagreement about Jacinta wanting to stay and Thomas wanting to leave. I remember she said, "If you want to go, you go!" and she had a little cry at the edge of the street.'

He said he took Jacinta for a ride on the buggy, then they returned to the party. He didn't mention her being injured or falling off the buggy at this stage. There were about ten people left at the party, including Corey, who had returned after seeing Jaye and the boys home.

Bengoa said, 'Jacinta asked for another rum. She was just floating around, socialising. Then she disappeared. Corey said, "I think I know where she is going." Corey and I walked past the carpark near the surf club.'

On their way, the two men came across Tom Davy, who was lying down in the rear of his car, and went to speak to him. Bengoa said, 'Thomas asked, "Where's Jacinta?" Corey and I said, "We are going to find her now." Thomas seemed a little agitated. I assume it was because he'd been sitting there on his own.'

Nothing is known of what the two men told Tom about his girlfriend's safety.

Louie said Corey seemed to know where Jacinta had gone. (How would he?) The three of them then walked to a house on the corner, a couple of streets further on. He said, 'It was a low-set house with no fence. I've never been inside it. I can't remember if lights were on.'

Bengoa's version differed significantly from Dean's. Dean said one or two men (he couldn't tell how many) drove by the first time and then went away. When they returned, there were three of them, and they came in the buggy. But Bengoa's version was that they only went there once and did so on foot.

He then said in his sworn statement that he moved away to have 'a leak and a smoke'. He hadn't gone to the door. He watched and heard events unfold from fifteen metres away.

'Thomas yelled, "Come on, Jacinta, it's time to go!" I heard another male voice yell, "Get out! Private property!"'

Bengoa said he couldn't hear if Jacinta was responding. He then heard a very loud noise, 'like a door was broken, and I thought *holy fuck!* and I was worried.' He said he started jogging around to the front of the house, where he could hear her screaming.

There were steps at the front, and Bengoa recalled, 'As I ran towards the stairs, Thomas came out. I saw blood on his shirt. He said, "Ring Triple-0." I said "What the fuck's happened? Where's Corey?"

'"Over there." Tom pointed towards the road, and I saw Corey lying face-up, not moving. Tom said, "He ran out."'

Tom managed to call Triple-0 before he collapsed, 'making a sort of gurgling sound', according to Louie.

Triple-0 was already on the phone inside, responding to Dean's call. The police and ambulance arrived quickly, but it too late to save Tom Davy or Corey Christensen.

Bengoa's statement ended with, 'I did not [have] any accidents in the buggy that night.' Why did he tack that on at the end of a nine-page statement?

◆ ◆ ◆

Detective Sergeant Neal also took Bengoa for an on-site walkaround. As they walked, Bengoa gave his version of why the men had focused on the house at 2 Topton Street.

He told Detective Sergeant Neal, '[We] thought obviously this would be the first place if she was to go somewhere, not knowing anyone, then we walked up from here.'

Neal asked, 'So did you come here just the one time or two times?'

'One time.'

'Only one time?'

'Yep.'

'So where did the buggy pull up?'

'Over near the trees there.' Bengoa pointed vaguely down the road.

'OK, once … Did you come here to the house at all first with just Corey?'

'I come past on my own and then went that way.'

'All right, so you went and got Corey and came back around?'

'I pulled up and saw Thomas.'

'Was it a situation that someone may have come up to the house first and then gone back to the buggy?'

'I'm trying to think. I think we all came together … I wouldn't have pulled up over here, more like over there near the last palm tree.'

'OK. Well, did you go inside the house at all?'

'No.'

'Have you ever been in this house?'

'Oh, years ago I have, yeah.' (This contradicted what he'd told Detective Hogan.)

Bengoa was vague about who had knocked and when. 'I don't know who went up there first, knocking, couldn't hear no response inside … and then Thomas said "Candice, I can see you. Come out, we'll go home" … I don't know if he could see her.'

Bengoa said he wandered about fifteen metres away for a pee and a smoke.

He said, 'I could hear Thomas going "Candice, come on, I can see you" and then getting noisier and noisier.' Tom was getting annoyed at Candice for not responding and acknowledging that he was there.

By this stage, the walkaround had brought them to a set of steps. Bengoa said, 'I think it was these steps I've walked up, and I saw Thomas … come out in a white shirt and it was all bloodied and he said, "Ring Triple-0."

'I didn't have my phone and I was a bit concerned about Corey, my mate, so I said, "Where's Corey is he still …" and Thomas said, "No, he's run, he's outside." Tom was pointing over there.

'I just went straight over there, and I thought he just must've … maybe fallen, hit his head, because he had a maroon Queensland shirt on. I couldn't see any blood until I got up close. Yeah, then I realised it was a bit more than just falling over. Then I didn't know what to do. Corey wasn't very responsive.

'A white car pulled up and two gentlemen got out and helped. They rang Triple-0. They were concentrating on Thomas, and I'm just holding Corey's hand ...

'I can remember the police coming. Then the detective asked, "How many people did you see?" And I said, "Just Thomas, Corey and the two other people."

'He said, "You didn't see anyone else?" and I said "No." He said, "Well, it must've been shock."'

◆ ◆ ◆

Bengoa told several versions of his story, but one thing didn't change. He was always just the driver.

He recalled hearing the other two shout rude comments when Candice didn't respond to their calls. He said, 'Then – I don't know how long, it just seemed really quick – I heard a bang. It wasn't glass breaking, I don't know if it was a window getting forced open or a door, and they entered the house.'

Police had arranged for Louie to watch a reconstruction of the events. They stationed him about fifteen metres from the door, where he said he'd been that night, then pulled and wrenched on the locked front door until suddenly there was a loud noise and the lock broke free.

'That's exactly the noise I heard,' Louie said.

◆ ◆ ◆

Later that day, Louie made a three-page statement giving yet another version of the lead-up to the stabbings. He'd now remembered that Jacinta had 'fallen out of the buggy at some stage. I recall that I did not play any part in her falling out of the buggy. I think she fell out herself.' He said he drove around in the buggy looking for her for a while, then went back to the party.

Corey was there, drinking with a few stayers. Louie told him that Candice had fallen out of the buggy and 'stormed off'. Drunk as they were, the two men decided 'to look for Jacinta, out of concern for her safety'.

He said that after picking up Tom while they were looking, he parked the buggy and they walked to Dean's house. So why did Dean tell the Triple-0 operator he could see *a buggy* carrying *three men*, at least two of whom broke into his house and put him in fear of his life? The recording speaks for itself.

A credible source informed me that Louie Bengoa had told a friend in the pub that he did enter the house, 'but I didn't do anything. I went straight out again.'

I've tried to reach Louie Bengoa, but he's changed his mobile number. His family is very protective, and his sister told me in no uncertain terms not to try again.

But the words he spoke in those conflicting statements and the videoed walk-through tell their own story. There are only three living witnesses to what happened that night. Did Bengoa move his buggy away from the house when, through all the beer and rum, he realised what a disaster the night was becoming?

He already had charges against him for driving under the influence. He must have realised that he could get done again for the same offence, at the very least. Maybe lose his licence, which is essential for a cane farmer. Is that why he told police the three of them arrived on foot? He's never answered that question.

At a police media conference on the Monday after the stabbings, Inspector Chris Lawson told the media he was trying to determine if the incident was 'a home invasion/self-defence, or a street-side fight'.

He said, 'It is extremely complex. We're dealing with a number of legal issues and we're also dealing with a number of people ... just to confirm what occurred prior to the incident. Self-defence is one of the options that we are looking at.'

He described the scene as 'harrowing – a horrific scene, to arrive there and find two people. We're talking about the dead of night, where it's totally dark.' People with terrible injuries were lying in the street.

He said this would 'obviously affect those people who had to go there and assist. There was blood there, and the effort they went to providing first aid to these people was fantastic.'

It may have been fantastic, but it was far too late. Forensic pathologist Dr Paul Botterill later told the inquest that the two men's injuries were barely survivable; they might just have had a chance if the injuries had been inflicted on the steps of a major hospital.

From the autopsy reports, it seemed that Dean Webber, jabbing a sharp fifteen-centimetre knife haphazardly in the direction of the intruders, had managed to deliver fatal wounds through the ribs of each men. He lunged with the knife twice, and each time had missed bone and cartilage and penetrated the pericardial sac around the heart, inflicting injuries that caused the men to suffer heart failure and bleed to death.

Both intruders had superficial cuts to their arms and face – Tom more than Corey, suggesting that Corey fled as soon as he was stabbed, while Tom put up a fight. The superficial injuries he sustained are loosely described as defence wounds, inflicted in the preliminary struggles.

For his part, Dean Webber had sustained bruising to his head, face and limbs. There were bruises on his neck consistent with finger marks and he also had injuries to his mouth. Neither intruder was armed with a weapon, but they could do quite a lot of damage, because they were both fit and very much bigger than Webber. Dean weighed only fifty-seven kilos, whereas Corey weighed eighty-four kilos and Tom 133.

The house was cordoned off as a crime scene for the next four days. The forensic investigation covered the lounge and kitchen areas inside and the porch and the driveway outside, down to the edge of the road. In the first forty-eight hours, the police examined all aspects of the stabbings. They interviewed Louie Bengoa, Candice Locke and Dean Webber in detail. Forensic people scrutinised the Webber house, and 'made a terrible mess' with their powders and potions, according to Dean Webber's father.

They found a spray of Tom Davy's blood on the fridge, and some of Corey Christensen's blood had been deposited on Davy as well as on the threshold of the door. Tom Davy bled more inside the house – 'a significant amount of the blood inside was his,' Detective Sergeant Neal told me later. 'Corey's injury caused him to mostly bleed internally, but droplets of his blood were found inside. The family argues there's not enough DNA evidence to place Corey in the house, but his blood was there.'

Significantly, there was *no* DNA or other evidence placing Dean outside, although the area outside the door was thick with blood. Dean had left no footprints. Detective Sergeant Neal told me later, 'This young guy has made two frantic calls to emergency, he's terrified and crying, pleading for help. Are we then to believe he mans up and goes outside armed, kills both trespassers and fakes the whole story, with Candice crouching in the kitchen?'

Neal told me, 'I believed what he said – there's no-one else who can tell us anything – and found he had no case to answer.'

This decision wasn't arrived at lightly. Under police regulations, a suspect who has been arrested can only be held for eight hours before being formally charged or released, although police can apply for a 24-hour extension if they need more time.

Dean was arrested about 1.30 am, so his eight hours were up at 9.30 am on Sunday. Neal applied for a further 24 hours, which he got, taking him until 9.30 am on Monday, which was a public holiday. During that time, police met repeatedly to discuss all aspects of the case.

Gavin Neal told me, 'You have to keep looking at every scenario, but our team couldn't find any evidence that contradicted Dean Webber's story of protecting himself because he was in fear of his life and Candice's. In that circumstance, it's permissible to use equal or more force to prevent grievous bodily harm or death. He was one slightly built young guy against at least two very big and angry men.'

Neal said, 'We never really considered homicide, but after we'd released him, the Brisbane Homicide boys paid us a visit. Two fatal stabbings and no charges? Once they'd seen the case, one of them said, "It's a pristine case of self-defence".'

◆ ◆ ◆

Brett Webber, Dean's father, was working on an outback property west of Winton when a friend rang and said he'd heard about the incident on the radio. Brett, who is a sort of super-handyman, packed up his tools and loaded the car. He set off immediately to drive the 720 kilometres to Townsville, where his lawyers thought it likely Dean would be taken to face a court hearing.

Dean's mother, who lived in Newcastle in New South Wales, caught a plane to Townsville, and they arrived at pretty much the same time, around midnight on Sunday. 'We hung around there for a while waiting to hear more from our lawyer, who was keeping abreast of things in Ayr,' Brett told me. 'Dean was still in the Ayr lock-up, but we thought he'd be coming to Townsville to get bail.'

Then they heard that Dean was going to be released on Monday after spending the night in the lock-up and giving a formal half-hour interview on tape without a legal representative's advice. They jumped in the car and drove to Ayr to meet him.

'It was pretty emotional,' Brett said. 'He was very glad to see us both.'

Later that day, after his release, Dean agreed to take part in a walk-through, returning to the house along with his father and sundry other interested parties, including police, recording techs and legal advisers. Looking small and vulnerable in a baggy white T-shirt, Dean stood in the middle of the messy lounge room, hugging himself and verging on tears.

He began explaining the events. At first, he was quite confident in his account, walking police through what happened when he got home from his evening with friends.

He explained that he was asleep on the couch, everything locked, no lights or TV on. 'Then I saw a lady standing at my door, saying "Help me, help me." I was a bit hesitant at first, but she was obviously injured, so I let her in, put her on the couch and got some ice to try to treat her. She said there were blokes following her, bad people, "Don't let them in. Ring Triple-0, we need police and an ambulance," she said. Then I saw the tail-lights of the buggy and I turned out the lights and rang for help.'

He said the men arrived – he thought only two of them – and started rattling the door, making threats. He told them several times to leave the property. 'They said, "Why should we leave?" and I told them, "I don't need a reason, just leave my property." Instead, they went all around the front and sides of the house, trying the flyscreens, looking for an entry point,' he told Detective Neal. 'I tucked Candice on the floor in the kitchen, as far out of sight as I could, because there are no curtains on the kitchen windows.'

After he made the first call, he said a policeman, Constable Dwyer, had rung him from Ayr and explained he couldn't attend immediately because he had someone in the watch house. 'He said, "Give Triple-0 a call if the scene changes." I begged him – "Please come as soon as you can."'

Then the buggy came back, this time with three or more men. He couldn't quite make out how many there were by peeping through a gap in the curtains. 'There was three of them I can see on foot because they got straight out and came over.

They started saying, 'Oh, where are you, dickhead? You know, don't call the police, you weak scum.'

Dean said, 'They had deep, threatening voices. That's when I got really scared. They injured her and now they're trying to get in – I was really scared. I didn't know what to do.'

He made the second call to Triple-0, but the operator was sceptical and didn't believe anything was wrong. Dean said, 'I thought that Candice and I would never walk out that door.'

As Dean moved toward the kitchen, he started to cry. He remembered, 'I was standing here, near Candice, and the first man ripped the door off. He said, "We've got you now, you little prick." For a third time, as the invasion seemed inevitable, he dialled Triple-O, while reaching behind himself for some sort of weapon. He said he felt a knife, which was usually kept with others in a knife block further along the bench, but it hadn't been put away from the washing up. 'I had a split second – oh my god – they're coming in! That's when they grabbed me, and in that time that's when they injured me, and that's when I was scared I was gonna die,' he said.

'I didn't know anyone involved,' Dean sobbed. 'I was just trying to help Candice. I just wanted to make sure Candice and I survived. Then three men came at me and tried to throttle me, and I just lashed out with the knife. I was in fear for my life. I don't remember anything … It all happened so quickly I had no time to react.'

Candice later gave evidence that she was crouched in the kitchen when she heard a scuffle in the open-plan lounge room. She heard 'shoving and grunting noises' but no voices. She had her head down and heard nothing to indicate that one of the men was her boyfriend, Tom.

Still gripping the phone, Dean said he'd stabbed 'a bloke who broke into my house'.

He told the operator he was still holding the knife he'd used.

The operator asked him to put it down. Initially, Dean said he wanted to keep it as evidence, but then he put it on the table.

When he turned on the lights, the emergency number recorded him sobbing uncontrollably as he surveyed the scene.

The audio then cut to police arriving and shouting at him not to move. 'The police told me to lie on the floor and then I got handcuffed and arrested,' Dean said, finishing his version of what happened the previous night.

◆ ◆ ◆

After that, the Webbers decided to take some time off as a family, effectively going into hiding to give Dean some time with them both and space to recover.

'When you live in a small town, it's pretty public,' Brett told me. 'Everyone was talking about it. We couldn't go to the shack anyway. It was crawling with police, and after them we had the forensic cleaners, who pretty much took the place apart. I told them I did not want a speck of blood left in the place.'

Before and after Dean's release, other witnesses who'd attended the NRL party were also interviewed. Tom Davy's mobile revealed the text messages sent to Candice on the night. They showed that until Bengoa and Christensen came to get him, Tom was unaware of Candice's plight and possibly considered their relationship over. Police also obtained copies of the Triple-0 tapes. As Detective Sergeant Neal told me later, they corroborated everything Dean Webber had told them.

After many hours of asking questions and getting DNA samples, police decided it was a genuine home invasion: Dean was in fear of his life and legitimately defending himself and a badly injured woman. At this point, they released him.

Gavin Neal explained that it became clear by early Monday morning that there would be no charges laid. 'Everything he said stacked up,' Neal told me. 'A team of police up to detective superintendent rank had been consulted. We had several round-table discussions regarding the stabbings before the decision was made to release Dean Webber without charging him with murder – or anything.'

Neal went on, 'We had two people dead. I kept asking myself, "Have I missed anything?" But Dean co-operated fully with us. Everything he told us was supported by the Triple-0 tapes, fingerprints and the other evidence from the crime scene, the witnesses and later the DNA – all that taken together gave us enough answers to be able to release him without charge.'

◆ ◆ ◆

Understandably, the families of the dead men weren't happy with the police decision. They contended that it was inconceivable that Corey or Tom would behave in this way. When Dean was released a couple of days after the incident, Detective Sergeant Neal described him as 'a genuine, honest young man from a good family who had acted in self-defence'. At this, the families became even more upset.

Tom Davy's family went public, saying they didn't believe Tom had invaded the house, even though his blood was everywhere. If he hadn't been in the house, how could anyone account for the blood spray matching his that was found on the kitchen fridge, near where Candice had been huddling? Tom's father Neil suggested that Dean may have armed himself in advance and ambushed Corey and Tom as they entered or approached the house. But there was no forensic indication that Dean had gone outside.

Neil Davy was at work when police arrived to tell him the news, twelve hours after the incident. 'I was completely devastated,' he said. The family was expecting Tom to fly down that morning to collect his dog, as he'd found a place in Cairns where he and the dog could live.'

On his way home, Neil called his daughter, Katie. 'It's critical,' he said.

'I thought it was Mum,' Katie told me. Her mother, Heather, is a cancer survivor. 'When I got home, I ran through the gate, and said, "Where is she?" Dad stopped me and said, "It's not Mum." There were so many people there ... I just thought, *No! Not my Tom. They have made a mistake.'*

But there was no mistake. Heather had already found out before the police told the family. The news had circulated so quickly on social media that her best friend found out before she did.

Tom's brother Josh, another big, good-looking young man, had phoned Tom that morning after he finished a shift at work, but Tom didn't answer. Josh thought he might be out on the reef fishing.

'We will never get over this,' Josh said after he found out. He said his brother was a 27-year-old man, in the prime of his life, with everything lined up ahead of him. 'And he was such a beautiful human. You just can't imagine a world without him in it.'

Katie said later that the family had been told by police that only Tom and Corey went into the house, and that they were unarmed. She said, 'We know Tom, and we know his one and only purpose would have been to help his injured new girlfriend.'

Heather supported this comment. 'How would you be,' she asked, 'if your girlfriend was in a dark house, injured, she's had too much to drink, and you don't know who is in there with her? You'd be worried and you'd want to get in and help that person you cared about.'

◆ ◆ ◆

Corey's wife Jaye Christensen said on national TV that her family couldn't comprehend why her late husband had to die.

Struggling to keep her composure, she said, 'He'd never hurt anyone.' Through her tears, she said he was a wonderful, kind father to the three boys left behind.

'We are hoping that those who are able to speak for themselves are truthful and give Corey and Tom's family friends and the Burdekin community a better understanding as to why their lives had to end this way.'

She disputed the idea that Corey had even entered the house. 'There was no DNA belonging to him found inside,' she said.

She called for an inquest as a 'plea for the truth. There's a man accused of killing my husband. It's important. People need to know it wasn't Corey. How did we get here? This sort of thing doesn't happen to people like us. It's devastating – unbelievable.

'I have no understanding of how this could happen. Corey was a fun-loving, average guy, a great husband and father, not aggressive at all. The children, while resilient like all kids, loved their dad and miss him. I am never going to let what has been said define Corey to his kids.'

Jaye said she was devastated when she was told how her husband lost his life. 'We don't know the full story,' she said. 'We want the truth and clarity around what has been said.'

◆ ◆ ◆

DNA is not the only evidence police rely on. For example, Candice had lain on Dean's couch when she first arrived, then moved to huddle in the corner of the kitchen. She was there for more than an hour, but none of her DNA was found in the house. There's a famous aphorism attributed to Carl Sagan: 'Absence of evidence is not evidence of absence.' Evidence that something is absent (for example, that we can show there are no elephants in the room) is significantly different from a simple absence of evidence (that we don't know if there are elephants because we haven't checked).

◆ ◆ ◆

Others in the community were still seeking answers about what happened. Several people felt the emergency response time had been less than satisfactory.

The Davy family disagreed with much of the information published about the night of Tom's death, but they were reluctant to say much publicly for fear of jeopardising an inquest. 'We have struggled with what has been in the media,' Josh said. 'It has been garbage. There have been so many different stories and no facts. But we have been quiet because we thought it might hurt the case.'

Katie added, 'Only three people really know what went down that night, and two of them are dead. It's that simple.' But it isn't quite that simple. Candice Locke and Louie Bengoa were both present, and they both survived.

'We're hoping it will go to an inquest,' Tom's mother said. 'No words can describe how much we will miss Tom. It is so heartbreaking to know how he has died. It just seems so senseless. It didn't need to happen. There are so many other scenarios that could have happened that night.'

Detective Sergeant Neal prepared a report for the coroner. He said that Dean Webber was a small man in fear for his own safety and that he told the intruders to leave on numerous occasions. Police had concluded that Webber's actions were justifiable in self-defence and the defence of Ms Locke.

◆ ◆ ◆

The task of the Coroner's Court is to determine facts, not guilt. It has rules that clearly set out the boundaries and capacity of its inquiries. It isn't bound by the rules of evidence but may inform itself in any way it considers appropriate. The court has quite sweeping powers to elicit information that may assist the outcome of an inquiry.

The principles were laid out in 1982 in the judgement on a controversial court case:

> An inquest is a fact-finding exercise and not a method of apportioning guilt. The procedure and rules of evidence which are suitable for one are unsuitable for the other. In an inquest it should never be forgotten that there are no parties, there is no indictment, there is no prosecution, there is no defence, there is no trial, simply an attempt to establish facts. It is an inquisitorial process, a process of investigation quite unlike a trial where the prosecutor accuses and the accused defends, the judge holding the balance or the ring, whichever metaphor one chooses to use.

It was almost two years before an inquest commenced into the events at Alva Beach. The terms of reference were to examine why no-one was ever charged with the fatal stabbings, and to review the emergency response to the incident by both Queensland police and the ambulance service.

Using her wide powers, deputy state coroner Jane Bentley called everyone who was in any way connected to the events on the night. Nineteen people gave evidence. The bar table was bristling with lawyers – some for the families and individuals, others counsel for the police and ambulance service. There were nine barristers, the same number of instructors, plus counsel assisting the coroner.

Early in the inquest, Dean Webber made a brief appearance by video link, looking composed, stating he didn't wish to give evidence on the grounds that it might incriminate him. The coroner excused him until later in the proceedings.

Detective Sergeant Neal spent more than six hours in the witness box, explaining why the police didn't attend faster and what happened when they did. The videos of the walkthroughs with Louie Bengoa and Dean Webber were shown. The court saw a weeping Dean wringing his hands and explaining what happened. He said in that video that three men jumped him and pummelled him to the ground.

Questions were raised about why Neal, a detective of about forty years standing, didn't have his gun, pepper spray or baton with him when he responded to the scene. Queensland police service procedures specify that a rostered police officer must carry these items while on duty.

Neal told me he felt hurt by this accusation. He explained to me that he'd initially been called back in to work after finishing his shift to serve arrest documents at the police station, but because it was so late, the JP had gone home. When things sounded as if they were escalating at Alva Beach, he went straight on to assist. Technically, he was still off duty.

Lawyer James Minnery, representing Tom Davy's family, said Neal's lack of accoutrements was a 'serious failure. At that moment, Neal knows he's responding to an incident involving a weapon ... where someone might be dead or dying. He knows there's a suspect still ... on the loose, and his response is to grab something which is not his accoutrements' – the paperwork opposing bail for the prisoner in the watch house – 'and then head off to that job.'

Ethical standards investigator Naomi Lockhart, who had reviewed Neal's response to the incident, agreed that aspect was a failure, but pointed out that Neal had been on a day off when he was called in to deal with the apprehended prisoner, who was sitting in the watch house. Neal thought he was on his way to get some papers signed, not to end up in a situation that could involve violence and death.

In any case, Troy Schmidt, speaking for the Queensland Police Union, said there'd been no breach of police policies or procedures. He argued that there was a distinction between rostered duty and overtime, where you're dealing with a specific matter that requires you to be recalled for duty. Mr Schmidt also suggested that part of the coroner's recommendations might clarify the obligations for police officers to carry equipment.

◆ ◆ ◆

The hearing also heard evidence from Candice Locke, now fully recovered from her physical injuries although still suffering emotionally.

She came to court with her father Martin, a former rugby league footballer who now owns a project home business in Townsville. He was devastated by the whole event. When I spoke to him nearly three years later, his voice broke with emotion when he spoke of his daughter's role and the impact the tragedy had had on the other living victims.

He was especially concerned about the Davys, but his lawyer had told him to have no contact with them. Some people were still not convinced about charges being laid. Even when legal advice is given for the right reasons, it can seem counterintuitive; the first instinct of the living victims of incidents like this is to comfort each other and offer support.

Martin's feeling of connection with the Davys was obvious, both having had children who suffered that night. Martin had told Candice that she must tell the coroner the absolute truth. I got the feeling he was big on telling the truth at all times.

Lawyers at the inquest asked Candice whether she was pushed off the buggy by one of the men or fell accidentally.

Candice told the court that because she was intoxicated at the time, she 'couldn't 100 per cent remember if she was shoved'. During her stay in hospital, her parents had instilled in her the importance of only giving evidence of which she could be absolutely certain.

She said she was in excruciating pain and felt scared when Mr Christensen and the other man refused to help her.

'They were laughing and I was quite distressed,' she told the coroner.

She told of getting off the buggy, seeking help at the first house she came to and then having a group of men start banging on the house and yelling her name.

'When Dean called police, we were advised to turn off the lights and hide. I was sitting there with my head down. I was really scared,' Ms Locke said. 'I was in the kitchen on the floor.' When she heard the struggle near her, 'it just sort of sounded like shoving or grunting and there wasn't really words being spoken'.

She said she didn't hear Tom Davy's voice during the struggle. It was only when police visited her in hospital the next morning that she found out her boyfriend was one of those who'd been killed.

As the inquest approached its end, everyone was waiting to hear from Dean Webber, the only person who really mattered to the grieving relatives. But their hopes were dashed. The court didn't hear from Dean but from his lawyer, who argued that he should be exempt from giving evidence because he continues to suffer severe post-traumatic stress disorder, and his condition would deteriorate if he was forced to answer questions about how Mr Davy and Mr Christensen died.

Deputy state coroner Jane Bentley at first insisted he give evidence in the public interest, but she then agreed he could do so in writing at a later date. In court, witnesses usually can't be forced to give evidence that may incriminate them, but coroners can issue a witness with a 'letter of comfort', which prevents them being prosecuted for a crime if they give evidence that incriminates them. These letters are provided at the discretion of the coroner where a matter of the public interest is involved. In this case, no letter of comfort was given.

Dean's treating psychiatrist said his patient couldn't discuss aspects of the incident without serious decompensation and risk of re-traumatisation. 'To subject Mr Webber to cross-examination is extremely dangerous, from a psychiatric point of view,' the psychiatrist said. 'Memory disturbance and suggestibility are features of PTSD, and aggressive cross-examination is likely to alter and distort his memories rather than allowing him to clearly recall what occurred.

Under cross-examination, he would almost certainly dissociate or emotionally decompensate and not recall an accurate recollection.'

After hearing these submissions, Bentley gave directions that Dean Webber be excused. She accepted the psychiatrist's opinion that giving evidence in person would cause him considerable psychological distress and exacerbate his post-traumatic stress disorder, meaning he would be unable to assist the inquest in any meaningful way.

◆ ◆ ◆

This ruling really upset the families of Tom Davy and Corey Christensen, who believed a rigorous cross-examination of Dean Webber was the only way to find out what really happened that night. Tom's uncle, a retired police officer in South Australia, said he believed somebody had to ask some hard questions of a man who had just stabbed two people to death. He said 'just writing them down on a piece of paper wouldn't cut it. You can't cross-examine him.'

Heather Davy said that it seemed easy for Dean to get a psychiatrist who listened to his side of the story. She said, 'He is having nightmares … scared about locking doors … had post-traumatic stress. Well, have a look at our little family. Our two children are both seeing someone, they both have nightmares. We can't sleep. We've had Tom taken from us so violently, yet we can turn up in court.'

So the families applied to the Supreme Court for a judicial review of Coroner Bentley's decision, requiring that Dean Webber not only provide written evidence but undergo testing by a court-appointed psychiatrist and be available for cross-examination.

This type of application requires money and fortitude. A Supreme Court challenge to a decision by an officer of an organisation that has unlimited funds to oppose the application is not a walk in the park for an ordinary person. The barrister for the coroner submitted that 'the argument for the applicants provides no textual analysis of the Act, nor authority to support the proposition that their right to cross-examine witnesses should prevail over the broad discretion reserved to the coroner. The fact that there are disputed facts does not create an obligation on the Coroners Court to call witnesses for examination or cross-examination.'

On the basis that the Coroner's Act gave Deputy Coroner Bentley sweeping powers and her decision fell within those powers, the application was dismissed in March 2020. The only avenue to appeal this ruling would have been through a higher court. Pursuing 'justice' can be very expensive. Just ask a lawyer!

◆ ◆ ◆

Coroner Bentley's formal finding, handed down on 6 October 2021, broadly supported Detective Sergeant Neal's decision that there was insufficient evidence to charge Dean Webber with any offence.

But the coroner was sharply critical of the police response when the crisis was developing. She found that the police had prioritised paperwork over responding to an emergency call, and that this could have contributed to the deaths of Davy and Christensen. If police had arrived half an hour earlier, the situation would most likely have been defused.

Ms Bentley also found that the subsequent inquiry by the Ethical Standards Command had 'failed to investigate in any depth or address appropriately' the police service's failure to comply with relevant policies and procedures and, significantly, the failure to give appropriate heed to the urgent nature of the incident', including the need to assist the ambulance service.

Ms Bentley also criticised police for not charging Louie Bengoa with driving-related offences, in spite of the evidence that he may have been driving under the influence of alcohol. When asked about the issue, Detective Sergeant Neal had said that he was preoccupied with the more serious aspects of the investigation.

She found that Bengoa was the only person who might have been able to give an account of what happened after Ms Locke entered

Webber's house, but she described him as an 'unreliable and unhelpful witness' who had tried to downplay his own role. She also doubted his evidence that he wasn't involved in the entry into Mr Webber's house and found he had 'no interest in Ms Locke's welfare or concern for her safety'.

She said, 'It is probable that, due to what he was told by Mr Bengoa, Mr Davy considered that it was necessary as a matter of urgency to remove Ms Locke from the house. It is probable that Mr Davy entered the house due to his false belief that Ms Locke required his assistance – possibly he believed that she was vulnerable due to her intoxicated state. Mr Christensen may have aided him due to his impaired judgement arising from his significant level of intoxication.'

The coroner also recommended that the police service review its response and other procedures. Overall, it was an inquest after which there were no winners.

◆ ◆ ◆

Whatever the coroner says or recommends, irreparable damage has been done. The families of the victims will never feel they have received justice.

And a young man living in a small community, about to begin adult life, has incurred a burden that will hang over his head, of having caused the deaths of two people. Fortunately, his family and friends have no doubt about his actions on the night and continue to support him.

The young diesel fitter, nineteen years old at the time, only survived because he found a fifteen-centimetre kitchen knife in the darkness and jabbed it haphazardly in the direction of the intruders. Dean Webber wasn't charged for the incident. It was deemed he acted in self-defence, protecting his own life and that of an injured woman.

Mr Webber's family has no doubt the teen would have been facing a double-murder charge had it not been for a fifty-minute recording of his Triple-0 call before the attack. Because the operator left the line open, the recording of the ordeal provided evidence to prove that he acted in self-defence.

His father, Brett Webber, told me that if the incident had happened a week earlier, that phone call wouldn't have been possible. 'We only had the landline phone installed three days earlier. Before, you had to stand out the front of the house to get mobile phone reception. He's incredibly lucky that way, but very unlucky the other way. It's a lot for a young bloke to deal with.'

Dean Webber has been seeing a psychiatrist and has been spending more time since that night staying at home. His father told me he is trying to get on with life as best he can, but knows the incident will be rehashed as every anniversary approaches.

In a small town like Alva Beach, it's hard to escape the whispers, but the Webbers look forward to closure and hope that everybody involved will have answers one day.

The young woman Dean helped, who castigates herself for drinking too much on that night and being the catalyst for the situation, has recovered from her ordeal. She is now living in another town, and her social media posts suggest she is getting on with life, although memories linger.

Jaye Christensen has moved south; she has set up a flower business in her new town and met a new man, although Corey will not be forgotten. Heather Davy, also a florist, remains angry about the way her beautiful son met his untimely death.

The families of Tom Davy and Corey Christensen continue to nurse nagging doubts about the behaviour of their loved ones on the night. Did they break in? Did they really set upon Dean Webber? How did a small man like Webber manage to inflict two fatal injuries in the dark? Why did their loved ones bleed to death with an ambulance half a kilometre away? Why did police take nearly an hour to respond to Dean Webber's desperate calls for help? Was there a police cover-up afterwards? Those questions are not easily put to rest.

Even today, several years after the incident, people found it hard to talk about this story. The collateral damage has been widespread and very painful. Unless Tom and Corey's families can forgive Dean Webber for his actions on that night, it's unlikely their anger will subside. And even if it does, they will continue to grieve.

Further reading

The judgement setting out the coroner's court's responsibilities is *R. v* South London Coroner *ex parte* Thompson at <https://swarb.co.uk/regina-v-south-london-coroner-ex-parte-thompson-8-jul-1982-2>

For the case against the deputy state coroner, see *Christensen and Anor vs Deputy State Coroner* at <https://archive.sclqld.org.au/qjudgment/2021/QSC21-038.pdf>

The inquest findings are at <https://www.courts.qld.gov.au/__data/assets/pdf_file/0011/697250/cif-christensen-cj-davy-it-20211006.pdf>

ABOUT THE AUTHOR

Robin Bowles is fondly known as Australia's True Crime Queen. She has been writing crime since 1997, when she read the story of the alleged suicide of Bonnie Doon housewife, Jennifer Tanner, and decided things didn't add up. She closed her PR business and set out to discover what had really happened. Robin writes about more than crime and investigation, although she is renowned for the forensic detail of her research. She writes about injustice and incompetence, and the pain and loss suffered by the survivors of crime, the living victims. Robin has written fifteen books and numerous short stories. She teaches writing and is in demand as an entertaining speaker about her work as a true crime writer. She lives in Melbourne with husband Clive and her Griffon Bruxellois dog, Chewie.

www.robinbowles.com.au
robinbowles@bigpond.com